VISIONARY

Gardens and Landscapes for Our Future

CLAIRE TAKACS

WITH GIACOMO GUZZON

additional writing and research
Hilary Burden

Hardie Grant

BOOKS

CONTENTS

USA

Glenstone

INTRODUCTION

The Gardens on Spring Creek

Chasing beauty and light in the world's great gardens and landscapes, framed through my camera lens for the past two decades, has enabled a rich life. Initially concerned purely with the aesthetics of gardens, my focus shifted to naturalistic planting, and now to a time when beauty alone, still essential, is no longer enough.

Visionary was born on a video call with James Golden (Federal Twist, USA), where Giacomo Guzzon, a mutual friend, also joined unexpectedly. Talking about ideas for my next book, it became clear from Giacomo, a London-based landscape architect and plant specialist, that our rapidly changing climate was the biggest issue the industry is facing. His expertise, curiosity, and ability to communicate the role of public landscapes and private gardens to help mitigate and address the effects of climate change, soon saw him join me on the journey to write and co-create this book's content.

Today the world is experiencing prolonged periods of drought, extreme temperatures, torrential rainfall, and flooding, which all necessitate new ways of planting and design – striving for more than just aesthetics.

I began photographing *Visionary* in June 2021, setting off on a three-month adventure across the Mediterranean, driving from the UK to Greece. Initially we envisaged I would photograph 30 to 40 gardens, however there was so much good happening, I just kept photographing and by the time I'd almost finished, two years later, we had reached almost 80 gardens – the last in Australia, close to where I grew up in The Dandenongs.

It has been the trip of a lifetime with countless adventures, driving across deserts in the US, to islands in Greece, through vast mountain landscapes in New Zealand, to the icy climes of Colorado and through record breaking heatwaves in the UK and Europe.

Being detained by police at Morocco airport for carrying a drone, and enduring intense negotiations with hackers in Copenhagen to retrieve my Instagram account, after driving all day across Germany, were all part of the experience.

This book represents a new aesthetic characterised by the optimism of people driven to work in kinder, more sustainable ways. It is a very exciting time to document. The good news is beauty – fundamental to our humanity – is still possible. There is beauty in accepting what is. In working within our environmental constraints while looking to the future.

I have learned that beauty lies in seasonality and in harshness. There is beauty in brown and in gravel. Beauty in car parks and hospitals, in educational facilities and public landscapes. There is beauty in restraint and wildness. There is also beauty in re-using and recycling industrial land, as well as the beauty in our gardens.

We are in a more conscious time, which calls for more conscious design and decisions. *Visionary* is proof of this.

ÁVILA GARDEN

**Designers: Renate Kastner and Miguel Urquijo
(Urquijo-Kastner Studio)**

Location: Ávila, Spain

A fifteen-minute drive from the medieval walled town of Ávila, Madrid-based landscape designers Renate Kastner and Miguel Urquijo have created one of their largest gardens, a beautiful sanctuary and a design masterpiece.

A private Mediterranean garden, Dehesa de Yonte sits above a large reservoir on rocky terrain surrounded by native holm oaks (*Quercus ilex*). Climate is defined by dry summers and occasional harsh winters with temperatures as low as −20 °C (−4 °F).

Urquijo-Kastner Studio used local stones leftover from the house construction and former quarries within the estate to create terraces with deep, free-draining soil to accommodate olive trees lifted from olive plantations in High Aragon, northeast Spain (where climatic conditions are more like Ávila's) to ensure a better chance of survival. Trees were selected with trunks to resemble the *Q. ilex* in the neighbouring fields.

Cupressus sempervirens, with their elongated forms, contrast beautifully with the olive trees. Plants including *Osmanthus heterophyllus*, *Arbutus unedo*, *Phillyrea angustifolia* and *P. latifolia*, were tested for hardiness and proved to be more robust than expected. Planting

in the early stages of growth is dominated by colour, scent and movement, but as the garden matures, the form and structure of woody plants become more prominent as they grow and fill the space.

This project pushes the boundaries of plant choices in cooler climates by trying new species outside their typical planting range. Urquijo-Kastner had no reference garden for learning and inspiration, so took risks, pioneering the use of atypical plants.

For the Madrid studio, 'A garden is a natural space; it is where nature is contained and controlled but nonetheless natural.'

At heart is the designers' love of nature, nurtured and respectfully maintained by Ávila's owners who equally love their garden.

In thinking about the future, Miguel and Renate believe gardens will be designed 'to be more respectful of the patterns, modes and elements that make up the landscape, and to continue to give pleasure and shelter by favouring our innate tendency to contemplate life and to heal our spirit'.

TOLEDO GARDEN

Designer: Fernando Martos
Location: Talavera de la Reina, Spain

This Spanish retreat sits in a quintessentially dry landscape, north-east of the city of Toledo, a UNESCO World Heritage site. The Toledo municipality has an exceptionally harsh climate, with high summer temperatures and low annual rainfall.

The property consists of a group of low-rise houses (originally livestock stables) and a traditional farmhouse. Locally sourced granite boulders give character and connect the garden to its rural location.

To the east, large windows and doors look out onto a garden bordered by a low dry stone wall, recalling its ancient agrarian heritage. In the distance, gentle hills are covered with evergreen oak trees – *Quercus ilex* and *Q. suber*.

Native and non-native planting design by Fernando Martos, assisted by Carlos Rodriguez Molina, is characterised by an array of herbaceous species, selected for their exciting textures as well as their ability to survive sporadic irrigation.

The only tree is *Acer monspessulanum,* a drought- and heat-resistant native species with semi-evergreen foliage. Prostrate rosemary is used for cohesion, grouped amongst the planting. The herbaceous layer consists of a matrix of *Sesleria* 'Greenlee', a low-growing evergreen grass of unknown parentage that acts as a filler plant. *Stachys byzantina*, with its distinctive creeping silver foliage, sits at the edges together with *Euphorbia seguieriana* and groups of mat-forming *Achillea tomentosa*. Vertical structural species are used in the middle of beds, such as *Salvia pratensis*, *S. officinalis*, Phlomis *viscosa*, *Achillea umbellata* and *Stipa gigantea* – this tall native grass is particularly evocative catching rays of light at sunrise and sunset.

LA GRANJA ALNARDO

Designer: Tom Stuart-Smith
Location: Ribera del Duero, Spain

Danish winemaker Peter Sisseck first approached English landscape designer Tom Stuart-Smith a decade ago to landscape La Granja Alnardo, HQ for his winery and modernist visitor buildings in Ribera del Duero, a famous wine region in Castilla y Leon, northern Spain.

The area, known more for its chalky soil than for its suitability for gardening, is subject to drought stress, which means an explosion of growth in the spring is followed by summer quietness when high temperatures and lack of moisture halt exuberance. Peter's site, on the south-facing slopes of the Duero Valley, is surrounded by gypsum cliffs covered with thin, free-draining stony soil and sparse low vegetation, posing challenging conditions for new planting.

Faced with a harsh environment, Tom's approach was to experiment, breaking out of his comfort zone. Instead of creating detailed planting plans, he opted for coloured diagrams, which are more visually intuitive and offered no language barrier for local vineyard workers who did the planting . Using a mainly native combination of seeding and planting, a dynamic, layered plant community was created. This process started by spacing out slow-growing trees and large shrubs, such as *Quercus rotundifolia* and several native junipers, then adding a loose matrix of quicker-growing, low shrub species such as cistus, santolina, salvia and rosemary, overseeding the area with drought-tolerant grasses, biennials and perennials for an ultra-naturalistic result.

Species were planted in the autumn to take advantage of prevailing moist conditions and cool temperatures. No water is used in routine maintenance beyond the establishment phase, nor are chemicals, fertilisers or imported soil used. Initially, all plants were sourced in a peat-free, loam-based mineral medium to facilitate their establishment. Now all plants are propagated on site through cuttings and seeds.

The 0.8 ha (2 acre) garden at La Granja Alnardo is maintained by Peter and one gardener, while Tom continues to visit annually to guide its evolution.

DEHESA EL MILAGRO

Designers: Clara Muñoz-Rojas and Belén Moreu (Muñoz y Moreu)

Location: Alcañizo, Toledo, Spain

Clara Muñoz-Rojas and Belén Moreu are founding members of the small, Madrid-based garden design studio Muñoz y Moreu. Their guiding philosophy is for a landscape to contain four essential qualities: beauty, silence, self-sufficiency and harmony.

Twelve years ago, they began their first large design project – one they're still guiding and nurturing – for the outdoor spaces of Dehesa el Milagro ('Miracle Meadow'), a 300 ha (740 acre) ecological farm in Alcañizo, a hamlet close to Toledo. The site is relatively flat and close to a river, surrounded by mountains, with deep sandy-loam soil and a few thickets of *Quercus ilex* trees. The farm model is designed to promote biodiversity by growing vegetables and raising animals through circular and rotational productive design – a closed, natural cycle. Owned and founded by businesswoman Blanca Entrecanales, it aims to set a benchmark for organic food production in Spain.

Clara and Belén were brought on to further the holistic principles of the venture, incorporating sustainability, low maintenance, and integration into the environment. Drought-resistant plant species well adapted to the climate were chosen, many of which were native. Gardens and courtyards were designed around new farm buildings, using local stone and recycled materials.

The heart of the garden, an interior patio, was inspired by Arabian gardens, using both water and shade to make it green and cooler – the temperature often exceeds +45 °C (113 °F). Aromatic and edible plants were used for inner courtyards, together with 'Pierre de Ronsard' roses and wisteria to provide shade. For the gardens looking outward, grasses such as *Stipa tenuissima* were chosen to change colour with the seasons and complement the landscape, merging with forms and tones typical of this part of Spain. Winding paths are bordered by a hedge of trailing rosemary; in contrast, *Agave americana* is scattered throughout the grasses.

In addition to the gardens, natural ponds were constructed using water from a large onsite well to support biodiversity and introduce riparian habitats for flora and fauna. Although this project was required to work as a productive farm, it was inspired by nature and the surrounding context. Clara and Belén worked with the land to maximise opportunities for biodiversity, while creating a beautiful, functional space and oasis for the community.

IBIZA GARDENS

Designer: Juan Masedo

Location: Ibiza, Spain

Juan Masedo, a garden designer from Ibiza, has constructed gardens since his early twenties when he moved to Can Frit, an estate in the island's south-east. Since then, he has developed his own style, creating natural gardens inspired by a passion for the island.

CASA BLANCA

When Juan first visited this private house enveloped by cliffs on the San Antonio coast, he felt it was like being on the bridge of a boat, with the site exposed to salt-laden winds.

The rocky landscape inspired an eclectic mixture of both native and non-native species. Prominent species in the garden are *Westringia fruticosa*, *Pistacia lentiscus*, *Teucrium fruticans*, *Arundo donax*, *Aloe arborescens*, *Agave attenuata* and *Limoniastrum monopetalum*. Planting areas are minimally irrigated during summer months and mulched with shredded organic material from the site to improve the soil and prevent erosion and dehydration.

At Casa Blanca, intentional yet organic lines and shapes are maintained with frequent clipping of shrubs in a bonsai-style treatment. *See pages 24-27.*

CAN PEP PUYOL

Can Pep Puyol is an old estate in the north of Ibiza, characterised by typical dry stone walls, terraces and pine forests covering the surrounding rocky terrain. Juan restored the terraces and re-created outdoor spaces for alfresco dining and relaxation. Terraced gardens adjacent to the main house step down the hillside expansively to the guesthouse below. Flat areas are made informal with meandering gravel paths constructed from local aggregate. Well-adapted, drought-resistant Mediterranean species include prostrate rosemary, *Helichrysum orientale*, and *Santolina chamaecyparissus*, while different varieties of ballota and achillea are arranged in a naturalistic style, creating a wild, lively setting. *See pages 28-31.*

LE JARDIN CHAMPÊTRE

Designers: Imogen Checketts and Kate Dumbleton

Location: Caunes-Minervois, France

Imogen and Kate, both professional horticulturists from the UK, fell under the spell of the south of France in 2013 while on a sabbatical year learning about Mediterranean gardening.

Taken by the wilder landscapes, they relocated to the medieval town of Caunes-Minervois in the Occitanie region to start Le Jardin Champêtre, a trial garden and plant nursery specialising in herbaceous plants.

With temperatures exceeding +35 °C (95 °F) in July, falling to –5 °C (23 °F) in January during occasional cold snaps, the decision was made to grow native species, with some South African plants for extra colour, and many ornamental grasses – plant species that would withstand the local climate without irrigation once established. To avoid limiting design opportunities, their chosen palette is not restricted to native plants. Large grasses are used to create shelter and shade for more delicate species. Calamagrostis, muhlenbergia, panicum, stipa, and sesleria are favourites among the robust grass species.

Their garden vision takes inspiration from the local scrubland garrigue landscape while blending with other elements from contemporary prairie-style plantings and English mixed herbaceous borders. Based on permaculture principles, they support plant biodiversity and practis e pesticide-free gardening.

Kate and Imogen connect their garden with the wider landscape using native woody plants such as *Arbutus unedo*, intermingled with ornamental grasses and perennial plants. To avoid colour clashes, plants are combined with bright flowers such as crocosmia (not typical of the region) with grasses (such as eragrostis) softening the colour and achieving a harmonious composition.

Plants are sparingly watered by hand; the nursery has no automated irrigation system or electricity. To minimise evapotranspiration, the soil is covered with gravel mulch or oak woodchips, a waste product from the local wine industry. Some vegetation is cut back to cope with extreme heat. Species like *Salvia pratensis*, santolina, helianthus, echinops and teucrium tolerate an early summer cut and will often re-flower at the end of summer.

LE JARDIN SEC

Designers: Olivier and Clara Filippi
Location: Loupian, Montpellier, France

Along the coast of the southern French region of
Occitania, near Montpellier, lies Le Jardin Sec,
a windswept, exceptionally diverse, experimental
garden and a Mediterranean native plant nursery,
Pépinière Filippi, created by Olivier Filippi and his
wife, Clara. The garden sits on the shore, overlooking
lagoons, oyster farms, and their home. Here they test
and showcase wild drought-tolerant, resilient species
they have collected in their travels over the years.
The climate in this area is harsh, with hot summers,
prolonged droughts, and cool and wet winters.

The site's severe climate combined with the
underlying clay soil creates, to the eyes of many, a very
challenging, nearly impossible scenario for a garden.
Olivier and Clara have travelled extensively for over
30 years, studying the habitats and flora of various
Mediterranean landscapes and understand how
plants have adapted to survive in extreme conditions.
This research has informed their selection of resilient
and visually attractive plants at the nursery and in their
garden, offering solutions for drought-tolerant garden
planting combinations in Mediterranean climates.
Olivier is also a prolific writer and has published several
books on creating dry gardens using robust species.

In Le Jardin Sec, plants grow in a deep gravel mulch
layer to drain the rainwater quickly while maintaining
some moisture in the summer. Some areas are lightly
mounded to provide even better drainage, so plants
grow on a dry surface, protected from mould and
diseases. Still, their roots can reach the moisture
accumulated in the lower levels below the gravel.
The result is an intricate mosaic of textures and shapes
reminiscent of the garrigue landscape. The central
area is covered with low-growing mound-shaped
plants, characterised by silver-grey to green foliage
and punctuated with vertical accents provided
by cypresses (*Cupressus sempervirens*). Some
prominent low species across the garden are *Euphorbia
rigida*, *Euphorbia ceratocarpa*, *Sulla coronaria* (syn.
Hedysarum coronarium), *Myrsine africana*, *Salvia
fruticosa*, *Cistus* x *purpureus*, *Phlomis purpurea*,
P. longifolia, *P. bourgaei*, *Stipa gigantea*, *Coronilla
minima*, *Catananche caerulea*, *Scabiosa minoana*,
Centaurea bella and *Teucrium fruticans*.

With the effects of climate change becoming more
pronounced, Olivier and Clara have created a garden
that offers inspiration and guidance for designing future
plantings that can withstand climate challenges, while
blending perfectly with the surrounding landscapes.
Their garden is also low maintenance: in these extreme
conditions only a few weeds can cope. Moreover, many
Mediterranean species produce allelopathic chemicals,
and by dropping their leaves, inhibit weed germination.

An important message of Le Jardin Sec (as the
name reveals), is to stop wasteful irrigation and embrace
the natural rhythm of Mediterranean landscapes, where
summer dormancy follows exuberant spring growth.

SOUTH OF FRANCE GARDENS

Designers: James Basson (Scape Design)
Location: Maussane-les-Alpilles, Grasse, and Tourrettes-sur-Loup, southern France

James Basson of Scape Design is an award-winning garden designer working with an international team of 'artist gardeners' specialising in creating sustainable, resilient gardens in the Mediterranean. He has lived and worked in southern France for over 20 years, obsessed by its natural landscapes and vegetation.

MAS DOU GAOU

The look and feel of this private garden in the foothills of the Alpilles draws inspiration from native Mediterranean vegetation growing on nearby dry, rocky slopes.

Soil topography is lightly modelled to create mounded beds, improving drainage for drought and heat-tolerant Mediterranean species. Planting beds are covered with 10 cm (4 in) of locally sourced gravel, allowing plants air circulation around the roots and preventing fungal disease.

Some species are replaced, while others are allowed to self-seed, creating a highly dynamic, fast-growing garden. The planting comprises two-thirds of mounding subshrubs and one-third of herbaceous species. Almond trees planted among the shrub-herbaceous layer connect the garden to surrounding orchards. *See pages 40-43.*

GRASSE GARDEN

Sitting among olive groves and orange orchards bordered by stone walls, the garden is characterised by deep, heavy and nutritious soil. For this reason, James embraces a greater percentage of resilient herbaceous species, allowing for a wilder look.

Areas around the house are 'tidier', with clipped shrubs, small, mowed lawns, straight lines, steel edges and dry stone walls, while further away forbs and grasses increase gradually, creating an agricultural feel – a distilled version of a prairie where species can collapse in heat and drought.

The garden is not irrigated, and a 10 cm (4 in) deep gravel mulch is used throughout the planted areas, helping to retain moisture and prevent weeds from seeding. While some people don't always embrace a wild look – especially in summer – this garden exemplifies a timely approach to designing and maintaining gardens. *See pages 44-45.*

TOURRETTES-SUR-LOUP GARDEN

James Basson created one of his first gardens, perched on a hillside, after relocating to France from the UK in 2000.

Their garden design strives for authenticity, in tune with its agricultural setting. Previously planted species, too ornamental for the site, were edited out, and typical dry stone walls and gravel paths were built with local stone.

Quintessential columnar cypress trees, olive groves and clipped low shrubs (rosemary, bupleurum and teucrium) are arranged in modern, informal patterns appropriate to a Mediterranean landscape, while introducing a loose, naturalistic style allowing herbaceous species to self-seed and others to grow naturally. *See pages 46-47.*

STAVROS NIARCHOS FOUNDATION CULTURAL CENTER AND PARK

Designers: Deborah Nevins & Associates and H. Pangalou & Associates
Location: Athens, Greece

Home to the Greek National Library and Opera, designed by Renzo Piano, the SNFCC was built on a derelict site (a former horse racing track) on the coast of Athens. Renzo's vision was to visually reconnect this part of Kallithea with Faliro Bay, restoring the broken link between urban and natural landscapes.

An artificial hill was constructed with the roof of both buildings emerging from it, creating a slope and concealing the view of the road below. Deborah Nevins & Associates and Helli Pangalou & Associates were assigned to landscape the 17 ha (42 acre) area, which took place over an eight-year period.

The 2.3 ha (5.6 acre) green roof over the library, opera and car park is the largest in Greece (and among the largest worldwide). Grasses and wildflowers were grown by local nurseries, from seeds collected by a team of researchers from the Diomidous Botanical Garden. Many mother plants were provided by well-known nurseryman Olivier Filippi, a specialist in dry gardens.

Soil depth decreases moving up the hill, while vegetation character changes as it would do naturally on a hillside, with herbaceous species at the top and woody plants at the bottom. Rich planting includes a total of 16 tree species and 161 shrub species. Rainwater is stored by the green roof, halving the building's energy consumption and reducing the heat-island effect. A photovoltaic canopy produces much of the energy used by the complex, providing vital shade.

SNFCC achieved the platinum Leadership in Energy and Environmental Design (LEED) certification, the highest level of green credentials in new construction.

Public areas feature water bodies, lawns, leafy avenues, diverse playgrounds and a vegetable garden. A large sea water canal connects conceptually with the neighbouring Saronic Gulf while storing stormwater. At the slope's base, water is stored and collected, reducing potential flooding. A desalination system provides additional fresh water for emergency irrigation during severe drought.

Adjacent to the canal, a pine–tree lined esplanade (paved with water-absorbing, recycled, self-binding gravel) bridges the coastal highway, connecting the waterfront.

A revolutionary precedent for public spaces in Greece, this international environmentally sustainable precinct changed the perception of native and drought-tolerant plantings in urban areas by elevating them, and contributed to making SNFCC one of the most important modern landmarks in Athens.

TATOI CLUB &
THE ROOSTER

Designers: H. Pangalou & Associates
Location: Athens and Antiparos, Greece

Founder of Athens-based H. Pangalou & Associates, Helli Pangalou has more than 25 years of international design experience, exploring predominantly landscape design and placemaking as dynamic ecosystems that inform, heal and enrich people's lives.

TATOI CLUB

Resorts, popular throughout the Mediterranean region thanks to mild winters and reliably sunny summers, are often excessively manicured, heavily irrigated, and planted with exotic species that don't follow the cyclical nature of endemic plants.

Times are changing. North of Athens, set among gentle hills covered with pines and other evergreen species typical of the landscape, Helli Pangalou has designed outdoor spaces for the Tatoi Club, a sports and wellness resort with 18 tennis courts, several swimming pools and low-rise buildings.

Soil from building work excavations was used to create landforms that direct and collect stormwater into a pond and swales. Lawns, reduced to a few key areas, were planted with *Dichondra repens,* which requires significantly less water; Mediterranean drought-tolerant and fire-retardant species were planted throughout the grounds. Local fine gravel was used to pave meandering paths and to mulch planted areas, reducing evapotranspiration during summer months.

After devastating wildfires in Athens in August 2021, the club took part in a reforestation initiative to replant over 1,000 trees and many more shrubs in the barren post-fire landscape, in the foothills of Parnitha.

THE ROOSTER

On the tiny Greek island of Antiparos, Helli Pangalou designed outdoor spaces for this new low-key wellness resort, the life's work of hotelier Athanasia Comninos. The Rooster sits on a sun-baked hillside facing Livadia Bay, among low, sparse garrigue vegetation dominated by aromatic and evergreen thornbush. The discreet, deeply considered retreat allows guests to feel absorbed into the landscape. Sixteen private villas and suites covered with green roofs were designed by Vois Architects.

Because of the wild and unspoilt setting, Helli's intervention focused on the landscape restoration of the construction site. Rainwater tanks were installed close to the houses, with drainage channels diverting stormwater into more ornamental plantings of fig and olive trees. Closer to the dunes, a limited number of native plants was introduced to enhance the existing flora with colours and textures emblematic of the place. Additional specimens of existing *Juniperus oxycedrus* were planted to amplify the tree's distinctive character, as well as *Sarcopoterium spinosum*, a native species reintroduced by local nurseries. More commonly seen with dark pink flowers, a cultivar of *Bougainvillea spectabilis* with pale salmon flowers blends in comfortably with the setting's aesthetic.

GREEK GARDENS

Designers: doxiadis+

Location: Athens and Antiparos, Greece

doxiadis+ is an Athens-based landscape architecture design team founded by Thomas Doxiadis, whose core principle is to see the world through the lens of 'Symbiosis' – a sense of exploration and respect for the intricate relationships between living things.

AMANZOE

The six-star Amanzoe Aman Hotel is an idyllic Greek Island holiday destination in the town of Porto Heli. The luxury resort's philosophy is to promote a feeling of being 'in the landscape' rather than looking at it from a distant standpoint.

Thomas Doxiadis' design approach features elements 'from refined to wild', inspired by local flora, such as pine tree groves and maquis scrub vegetation, with others derived from agrarian traditions, including sinuous dry stone walls, olive tree plantations and vineyards. Sustainability is met in low irrigation needs for vegetation and the recycling of materials found or produced on site during construction.

The hotel showcases diverse and richly planted roofs on the cabanas, pavilions and villas, with resilient mound-forming shrubs that blend with forms and colours of the surrounding landscape. In the main entertaining areas, pathways are lined with ornamental grasses, such as *Stipa tenuissima*, and tall slender cypress trees are a striking feature.

LANDSCAPES OF COHABITATION

This development project, consisting of 32 villas on the island of Antiparos in the southern Aegean, offered doxiadis+ an opportunity to address the trend of destructive development in the tourist economy, with design sympathetic to both natural environment and cultural heritage.

It is important that some developers are working with landscape architects who ask the question: 'How does one build on the stark beauty of a Cycladic landscape without destroying it?'

doxiadis+ used existing terraces and dry stone walls as guiding lines for new roads and housing locations so as not to disfigure the hillside. Man-made elements such as *pezoules* (terraces created on the hillside for agricultural purposes), and *xerolithies* (dry stone walls) reflect the island's ancient agricultural history.

Indigenous plant species were incorporated to blur boundaries with surrounding vegetation. New plants were used in mixes rather than in blocks, allowing them to intermingle for a more natural effect. Species were planted at different densities throughout the site – the highest at the centre, the lowest at the perimeter – leaving more empty spaces and encouraging natural revegetation. New villas were inspired by traditional local architecture, although unconventionally built; recycling and re-using building materials and adopting green roofs as insulation.

AMSTERDAM PUBLIC PLANTINGS

Designers: Ton Muller and the city municipality of Amsterdam

Location: Amsterdam, Netherlands

Above: Vivaldi

Ton Muller, a Dutch landscape architect working for the city of Amsterdam's design office, creates robust plant communities for urban environments. Working for the city allows him to influence its green and design policies, while his designs for public spaces provide a model for future cities. Ton recently started a planting design program to teach young designers how to design with plants in cities.

ZUIDAS BIOSWALE

Amsterdam usually has more than enough fresh water due to normally well-distributed rainfall throughout the year. However, severe summer droughts are increasingly common and more solutions for greening the city are needed. Here, Ton designed rectilinear rain gardens to collect stormwater from adjacent pedestrian pavements. The woodland-edge plant community features trees, shrubs and herbaceous species that create a vegetation system capable of coping with fluctuating soil moisture levels during summer and inundation at other times.

Ton uses mixed plantings (native and non-native species) to bring nature into the city, selected according to needs and habitats. He stresses the need to shift aesthetic models of maintained plantings towards those with a wilder look, allowing plants to intermingle and evolve – a fundamental pivot for urban areas. *See page 70 (bottom)*.

ORLYPLEIN

The concourse of Sloterdijk station was converted from a concrete transit hub into a green square, featuring planting areas providing seating and refuge for commuters. The central part of the square sits on a slab above train tracks and has minimal soil depth, presenting challenges for species selection and long-term performance. Ton's design is composed of small multi-stem trees such as *Crataegus coccinea* and *Amelanchier lamarckii* scattered among a mixed layer of herbaceous perennials and grasses. Prominent herbaceous species include asters, amsonia, *Hemerocallis citrina*, *Anemone x hybrida* 'Richard Ahrens', sedum, *Phlomis russeliana*, *Sesleria autumnalis* and a variety of geraniums. *See page 71 (bottom) and pages 72-73*.

Above: Beethowenplain

NETHERLANDS GARDENS

Designer: Arjan Boekel
Location: Heiloo and Landsmeer, Netherlands

Arjan Boekel is a Dutch landscape architect working mainly with plants to create naturalistic outdoor spaces. He believes 'the garden as a habitat' is a vision reflected in all our gardens.

HEILOO

Arjan's landscape design for this parking lot in a mental healthcare facility in Heiloo, a small town north of Amsterdam, features an extensive system of gardens for rainwater collection and stormwater management. Planting beds are slightly sunken, and sandy soil below the rain gardens allows rainwater to infiltrate naturally.

Planting design responds to different moisture levels across the swales: moisture-loving species are planted in the lower sections, with more drought-tolerant species on the ridges. Airy planting allows for connectivity throughout the parking area, forming a transparent buffer zone between old and new buildings.

Trees and shrubs were chosen for high pollen and nectar production, as well as their stunning autumn colour and attractive shapes. Key woody species include *Salix elaeagnos* ssp. *angustifolia*, *Cornus sanguinea* 'Winter Beauty', *Viburnum opulus*, *Clethra alnifolia*, *Aronia melanocarpa* 'Hugin' and *Cephalanthus occidentalis*. On higher ground *Euonymus alatus*, *Hydrangea quercifolia* 'Burgundy', *Hedera helix* 'Arborescens' and *Itea virginica* 'Henry's Garnet' is intermingled among the herbaceous layer.

Herbaceous planting features three different mixes according to their location within the swales. Down in the swale is a matrix of *Iris sibirica*, interplanted with *Sanguisorba officinalis*, *Deschampsia cespitosa*, *Filipendula vulgaris*, *Lythrum virgatum* 'Dropmore Purple' and *Cirsium rivulare* 'Atropurpureum'. Around the slopes and edges, groups of *Echinops bannaticus* 'Blue Globe', *Bistorta amplexicaulis* (syn. *Persicaria amplexicaulis*), *Cenolophium denudatum*, *Veronicastrum* 'Red Arrows', *Amsonia tabernaemontana* 'Storm Cloud', *Phlomis russeliana*, *Rudbeckia fulgida* var. speciosa, *Helenium* 'Rubinzwerg', *Pycnanthemum tenuifolium* and *Sesleria autumnalis*.

Baptisia 'Purple Smoke' makes large domes in the more drought-tolerant spots, randomly interplanted with *Echinacea pallida*, *Sesleria autumnalis*, *Molinia caerulea* ssp. 'Edith Dudszus', and tufts of *Phlomis russeliana*, *Anaphalis margaritacea* and *Calamintha nepeta* ssp. *nepeta*.

LANDSMEER

Arjan created this immersive, wild and intimate private
garden in Landsmeer, north of Amsterdam, for its
owners to be embraced by plants and observe nature.

The property has a natural swimming pond and
a flowering meadow area. The meadow was planted
for a long flowering season with a mix of mainly
Eurasian steppe-plants and North American prairie
perennials. In the following years, planting was filled in
with native plants such as oxeye daisy, white campion
and wild carrot allowed to self-seed and grow wild in
the garden. At the garden edges, woody plants create
a buffer and filter wind from across the polder while
allowing a visual connection with the rural landscape.
Native and non-native plants, wet and dry habitats,
and environmentally friendly maintenance practices
attract a wide variety of insects, amphibians and birds.
In contrast to neighbouring conventionally maintained
plots, Arjan has created a biodiversity refuge.

ALMERE

Designer: Lianne Pot

Location: Almere, Netherlands

Lianne Pot is a garden designer and owner of Lianne's Siergrassen, an herbaceous perennial nursery and prairie-inspired show garden near Groningen in the northern Netherlands. Her fascination with prairie plants was sown by a visit to wild prairies in the US, where she observed North American species forming stable plant communities with deep roots, withstanding drought and out-competing weeds.

The 0.35 ha (0.8 acre) private family garden, built on reclaimed land below sea level in the planned city of Almere, is representative of Lianne's approach to evolving gardens towards a more durable, environmentally friendly design.

Lianne worked closely with the garden owners, enabling them to feel a part of the project, and better equipped to maintain it. A plan was developed for the plot, and planting out by the owners was completed with Lianne's support.

The low maintenance garden, where no pesticides or herbicides are used, became an oasis buzzing with insects; a place to sit, relax and observe. Plant species support each other and work together in a close-knit community. After the establishment phase, watering was no longer necessary. The site's clay soil has excellent water retention, with many species chosen for their deep root systems.

This project shows how even landowners on small plots can positively impact their environment.

NIEUW-HAAMSTEDE GARDEN

Designers: Piet Oudolf, in collaboration with Tom de Witte

Location: Nieuw-Haamstede, the Netherlands

Nieuw-Haamstede's coastal location south of Amsterdam is characterised by salt-laden winds and sandy soils. Here, visionary Dutch planting designer Piet Oudolf, a leading figure of the 'New Perennial' movement, has designed a private garden and a series of green roofs over a timber-clad house and garage. Tom de Witte, a Dutch garden designer and Piet's friend, collaborated with him on this project and was involved in the construction phases of the garden.

The green roofs are covered with a 15 cm (6 in) layer of manufactured lightweight, free-draining substrate, creating an environment for drought-tolerant species which prefer lean, light soils.

With increasingly unpredictable weather patterns, Piet selected sturdy species that could tolerate coastal winds. Sunny plant community members include achillea, *Allium tanguticum* 'Summer Beauty', *Amsonia hubrichtii*, *Calamintha nepeta*, *Eryngium bourgatii*, *Limonium platyphyllum*, lavandula, *Salvia yangii* (syn. *Perovskia atriplicifolia*), *Sesleria autumnalis*, sporobolus, echinacea, *Teucrium x lucidrys*, agastache, *Origanum laevigatum*, *Salvia sclarea*, *Sedum* Matrona, *Stipa tirsa*, *Stachys byzantina* and *Festuca mairei*.

An irrigation system (equipped with a sensor responding to variable weather conditions) was incorporated to establish the plants.

COPENHAGEN LANDSCAPES

Designers: SLA

Location: Copenhagen, Denmark

Stig L. Anderson is a visionary Danish landscape architect, founder and creative director of Copenhagen-based SLA, a nature based, interdisciplinary studio working with landscapes, urban spaces and planning. From city-wide masterplans to neighbourhood pocket parks, SLA's philosophy is to 'design places for life'.

AMAGER BAKKE COPENHILL ROOFTOP PARK

Completed in 2017, CopenHill is the world's first combination ski slope and waste-to-energy power plant, turning technical infrastructure into a social, sustainable and biodiverse asset for the city of Copenhagen. The building was designed by the Bjarke Ingels Group (BIG), who define themselves as 'future form givers', operating in line with the United Nations' '17 Sustainable Development Goals'.

The sizeable 1.5 ha (4 acre) tilted roof hosts a 500+ m ski slope, hiking trails, playgrounds, climbing and other sports opportunities, all with spectacular views of Copenhagen's coastline. On and around the ski slope, SLA planted more than 300 wind-resistant, drought-tolerant trees, and 7,000 shrubs among a carpet of grasses and wildflowers.

CopenHill's unique position and orientation creates an entirely new, exposed ecosystem for Copenhagen, not to mention a popular new 'mountain' to climb for residents more accustomed to the city's flat terrain. In the words of *Fast Company*'s review of the project, 'Why not try to have some fun when you're trying to go carbon-neutral?'

In monitoring vegetation species' diversity and richness on site, SLA biologists found an exciting increase in new species only a couple of years after construction.

SANKT KJELD'S SQUARE / BRYGGERVANGE

With the increased threat of flooding due to climate change, alleviating pressure on outdated urban water infrastructure is critical. SLA have created a precedent for sustainable urban drainage systems and climate adaptation measures in Copenhagen, by transforming a conventional roundabout and street corners into a small ornamental forest.

Such an intervention has improved the local microclimate by reducing pollution and controlling the urban heat-island effect. The forest acts as a stormwater sponge by combining water retention features with planting, maximising opportunities for biodiversity. Stormwater is conveyed into a meandering series of heavily planted rain gardens that collect and slow down water, protecting the neighbourhood from potential flooding.

Prominent woody species include *Taxodium distichum*, swamp cypress, pine, maple, dogwood and willow species, *Aronia melanocarpa*, and *Corylus avellana*.

SLA's founder Stig L. Andersson calls this 'City Nature' – man-made nature designed not merely for how it looks, but also for resilience and biodiversity.

KLINTA GARDEN

Designer: Peter Korn

Location: Höör, Sweden

Peter Korn and his partner Julia Andersson are creators of Klinta Garden (Klinta Trädgård), a mesmerising private garden and nursery located in a typical Swedish landscape of rolling fields and broad-leaved trees, north of Lund.

Peter is a nurseryman and landscape designer known affectionately as 'the Sand Man' – a pioneer of growing in sand, a methodology that produces well-developed root systems, requires less irrigation, and makes plants easy to harvest throughout the year.

At Klinta Garden, areas with naturally sandy soil were made even more free draining by adding sand. Crushed sand, being easily compacted, prevents insects from digging into it and building their nests. Glacial sand, with rounded particles, remains friable and is more beneficial for invertebrates.

A self-confessed 'plant geek', Peter started growing plants for his nursery business more than 15 years ago, and now grows plants for his projects only. He has a fascination for wild plant communities in steppe regions worldwide, recreating their environmental conditions so they can thrive. Peter and Julia grow many plants that occupy specific ecological niches and habitats by changing the topography and making soil conditions more extreme.

Klinta Garden has an exceptional concentration of species that form different communities sharing the same environmental needs, resulting in impressive, colourful compositions of herbaceous plants and grasses with a very long flowering season. *Dianthus carthusianorum*, *Stipa pulcherrima*, and species of baptisia, salvia, ballota and echinops intermingle in central areas of the garden. Woody plants are used mainly on northern sides and edges of the property to prevent shading of sun-loving plants.

Understanding plants fully is important to Peter who believes that with inspiration from the wild, 'it is possible to create low maintenance plantings with high diversity in almost any environment' – essential in cities where plant resilience is tested under challenging conditions and lack of maintenance is common.

MAX IV LABORATORY LANDSCAPE

Designers: Snøhetta

Location: Lund, Sweden

MAX IV Laboratory is part of a larger transformation of an area northeast of Lund, turning agricultural land into a 'Science City', with the creation of a green public park.

FOJAB Architects planned the building (a next-generation synchrotron radiation facility) while the design of the surrounding 19 ha (47 acres) of land was conceived by Snøhetta, a Norwegian-based interdisciplinary firm devoted to architecture, landscaping and other design disciplines.

The landscape is designed to support the performance of the laboratory by creating a hilly terrain that secures mass balance on site and mitigates ground vibrations from the nearby highway. Mounds, made from soil excavated from the building's foundations, unfold from the circular architecture into the landscape in a radial arrangement meeting a spiral movement.

A meadow of native species features in the rolling landscape, varying across the site with different plants inhabiting dry, more exposed ridges, while others thrive in the moister conditions of low-lying areas. Managed by sheep grazing and conventional machines, the expanse is also designed to harvest stormwater in ponds and provide grassy habitat for wildlife. The building itself hosts a vast green roof composed of hylotelephium (syn. sedum) species.

While research institutions are more often fenced off and inward-looking, the dramatic juxtaposition of a high-tech facility within a natural realm sets new standards for their design.

JAKTGATAN AND LÖVÄNGSGATAN, NORRA DJURGÅRDSSTADEN

Designers: AJ Landskap

Location: Stockholm, Sweden

The new district of Hjorthagen, built on a former gasworks site, is due for completion in 2030. Jaktgatan and Lövängsgatan streets, constructed in 2015, form the main green link in the western parts of Norra Djurgårdsstaden. The city of Stockholm has ambitious and visionary goals for this repurposed neighbourhood, using thermal power stations with bio-based fuel, equipping all roofs with solar panels, and providing charging points for electric cars.

Ecological links improve biodiversity: a system of green streets and parks weaves together existing and newly created areas of nature among residential neighbourhoods and industrial artefacts. The fossil free project leads the way in innovation and livability in the capital, with green plazas, pocket parks, rain gardens, and extensive tree planting.

The rain garden takes stormwater from the adjacent pavement while irrigating layered naturalistic planting. The garden features multi-stem and single-stem trees, providing year-round display, celebrating Stockholm's four distinct seasons. The stunning autumn foliage of *Cercidiphyllum japonicum* adds another layer of interest, filling the air with sweet scent. Narrow wooden boardwalks and platforms with seating enable visitors to experience the rain garden from the inside.

GERMAN GARDENS

Designer: Harald Sauer

Location: Ludwigshafen and Mannheim, Germany

Harald Sauer is the head gardener of Ebertpark, a public park opened in 1925 for the South German Horticultural Exhibition in Ludwigshafen. This city, known for its chemical industry, sits on the Rhine riverbank opposite Mannheim, where, as a planting design consultant, Harald was involved in an extensive intervention at the Luisenpark. In his work for the city Park Department, Harald gained a reputation for designing extensive habitat-based plantings in public spaces.

EBERTPARK

Dating back to the 1960s, Quellgarten in Ebertpark, Ludwigshafen, had become dilapidated and consisted of plants requiring considerable care and constant irrigation. Harald's massive garden redesign in 2012 (phased in seven steps from 2012 to 2019), has transformed a dated park into a perennial dreamscape, with an open prairie area and woodland edges. Spacious beds are planted generously with robust species featuring attractive seedheads and winter silhouettes and require little maintenance and water. *Romneya coulteri*, *Albizia julibrissin* 'Summer Chocolate', *Miscanthus nepalensis*, *Nepeta racemosa* 'Walker's Low', *Amsonia tabernaemontana*, *Bupleurum fruticosum*, *Glycyrrhiza yunnanensis* and *Datisca cannabina* are used in the sunny habitat. The project has elevated Ebertpark residents' daily experience of their city. *See pages 104-107.*

LUISENPARK

Luisenpark is Mannheim's central park, built in 1975 for 'BUGA' (short for Bundesgartenschau), Germany's biennial federal horticulture show. For BUGA 2023 (and ongoing), Harald redesigned Luisenpark's main entrance – traditionally planted with annuals – as if in a dream. Developed with the park's horticulture director Ellen Oswald, a completely re-imagined re-design featured a sustainable planting approach using drought-tolerant species that required less maintenance while conserving natural resources.

A perennial meadow displays a combination of block and mixed planting with drought-tolerant species including *Patrinia scabiosifolia*, *Stipa tenuissima*, *Dianthus carthusianorum*, *Iris domestica*, *Sporobolus heterolepis*, *S. airoides* and *Sesleria autumnalis*, *Silphium terebinthinaceum*, *Stipa gigantea*, *Eryngium agavifolium*, *Muhlenbergia rigens*. Other large species were used in small groups as accent plants. Within the herbaceous layer, robust shrubs (such as *Cotinus* 'Grace', *Indigofera amblyantha* and *Bupleurum fruticosum*) were planted for year-round structure and stature. *See pages 108-109.*

RUIN GARDEN

Designers: Anselm Reyle, Tanja Lincke, and Das Reservat

Location: Berlin, Germany

Public parks have been created in disused industrial settings for decades, from the Bethlehem SteelStacks in Pennsylvania (USA) to the Landscape Park Duisburg Nord in Germany. However, private gardens displaying this approach are less common, though equally important.

Ruin Garden (Ruinengarten) represents a powerful example, challenging the typical aesthetic of a private garden and embracing the derelict beauty that can be found in urban areas. Located in a former shipyard on the banks of the Spree in south-east Berlin, the land formerly occupied by East German water police was abandoned after reunification in the late 1980s.

Inspired by New York's High Line, the garden is a collaboration between artist Anselm Reyle and his wife, architect Tanja Lincke (designer of their onsite house), with planting design by Berlin-based landscape architects Das Reservat. A warehouse was artfully deconstructed to create room for the garden and to visually link the house on one side of the property with studios on the other. Materials were left in their original condition and, sometimes, place. The result: a bold, authentic atmosphere.

Concrete and steel (with high carbon contents) are re-used – a sustainable approach aimed at minimising the project's carbon footprint. Ruderal vegetation grows among concrete debris, framing views and softening edges. Woody plants were chosen for their ability to grow spontaneously in abandoned wastelands. *Betula pendula* and *Rhus typhina* are placed throughout to create living, vertical elements, intermingled among an airy, lower layer of deciduous grasses and herbaceous perennials with different textures and heights. Shrubs are used sparsely to add structure and mid-level stature.

All species have an uncultivated look, as if they had self-seeded and always been there. The red stems of *Cornus sanguinea*, orange berries of pyracantha and white birch trunks form an artistic composition, especially in autumn.

Ruin Garden reflects the functionalist principles of German industrial designer Dieter Rams, who believes that good design is innovative, honest, aesthetic, unobtrusive, and environmentally friendly.

AZAREN

Designers: Eric Ossart and Arnaud Maurières (O+M)

Location: Tnine Ourika, Morocco

Azaren ('fig tree' in local Berber language) is the secluded retreat of English owners Lilian and Christopher Fawcett in the Moroccan High Atlas.

In 2008 architect Imaad Rhamouni designed the contemporary house (plus pool, guest pavilions and service buildings) in a typical ochre colour. Three years later, Paris-based Eric Ossart and Arnaud Maurières were appointed to ground the buildings into the landscape. O+M have designed more than 100 gardens in France, Spain, Morocco, Tunisia, Egypt, Syria, Mexico, and Japan, and are internationally known for their striking environmentally sensitive landscapes in often dry locations.

Azaren in the Ourika River Valley has fewer extreme temperatures than Marrakech further north, and fertile, irrigated soils more suited to agriculture. An orchard of roughly 8 ha (20 acres) is cultivated with olives, pomegranates and fig trees.

The ochre colour is a defining component, linking buildings to earth tones of the surrounding landscape and traditional architecture. Similar hues in different materials were used to construct steps, walls, and paths.

Planting is a variation of a steppe style, the combination of native and trialled non-native species, selected to be attractive and well-adapted to the conditions. *Agave sisalana* is used generously throughout the garden, intermingled with other agave cultivars, cacti and ornamental grasses.

The sloping terrain is modelled to create four low terraces rising from the main building up to the swimming pool, emphasising the view of the Atlas Mountains in the background. Further away from the buildings, the agrarian theme dominates with fruit trees connecting the garden to nearby agricultural fields.

KNEPP CASTLE ESTATE

Designers: Tom Stuart-Smith, James Hitchmough, Mick Crawley

Location: West Grinstead, West Sussex, England

Knepp Castle Estate spans several pioneering eras, from its 12th century castle ruins to the 19th century mansion designed by John Nash, a leading British architect of the Georgian and Regency eras. Today's estate, owned by Charlie Burrell and his wife, writer Isabella Tree, has embarked on a new era as a rewilding project, ecotourism destination, and regenerative farm committed to producing high-quality meat and vegetables while safeguarding the soil and environment.

It is also the centre of a high-profile gardening experiment: part of a scientific, ecological and educational project aimed at finding ways to maximise biodiversity across the estate. Knepp Castle Estate's scientific committee generates ideas in rewilding once-conventional gardens. Members include designer Tom Stuart-Smith, estate head gardener Charlie Harpur, emeritus professor in Plant Ecology at Imperial College Mick Crawley, and emeritus professor in Horticultural Ecology at the University of Sheffield James Hitchmough.

Rewilding techniques typically used on large-scale landscapes are not always practical or easy to apply to a garden setting, but the gardens at Knepp are being used as small-scale examples to demonstrate the rewilding effect on biodiversity.

In the wild, natural disturbance through soil movement and topography alteration is done by large animals; in the gardens it is replicated by humans through pruning, digging and planting. Plants are pruned into topiaries by Charlie ('chief disturbance agent') mimicking continuous browsing by large mammals. Disturbance keeps ground conditions in a constant state of change, increasing spatial complexity and ecological niches for wildlife. Weeding is not a term used at Knepp; instead, gardeners practice selective grazing to limit the expansion of certain species.

A large flat lawn was removed in the walled garden, making way for uneven terrain with different soil moisture levels to help improve habitat and floral diversity. Recycled crushed concrete and sand reduces fertility, altering topography to create dry ridges and low, damp areas where rainwater can collect in the winter and generate ephemeral pools. More than 600 native and non-native species were planted, watered only in the first year of establishment. Natural succession and self-seeding are encouraged, contributing to the garden's dynamism and complexity.

A traditional lawn and raised beds were removed from the kitchen garden, and converted into no-dig plots with 'dirty' paths where plants could creep in. These were covered with a 10 cm (4 in) layer of crushed limestone aggregate and planted with herbs and drought-tolerant species.

Knepp Castle Estate is a unique experiment and an important project for anyone interested in gardening more sustainably, embracing a new aesthetic – especially for England. It teaches us how plants deal with stress and disturbance – even more relevant when facing a future of extreme and unpredictable weather patterns.

WUDSTON HOUSE

Designer: James Hitchmough
Location: Wedhampton, Wiltshire, UK

For over three decades, planting designer James Hitchmough has been a leading, international figure in the ecology, design and management of herbaceous vegetation, producing a large volume of research on native and non-native meadows, steppe and prairie vegetation, sown in situ.

For the owner of Wudston House, David Morrison, James created a novel meadow plant community in a lawn that is dry in summer. Drought-tolerant species from American prairie, South African and Euro-Asian origins are combined; species from different biomes with similar climates share some characteristics that make them compatible, even if they developed in distinct continents.

Most species were seeded in 2012 in 10 cm (4 in) of sand to lower the nutrient levels in order to prevent weeds from overwhelming the perennials. A few slow-growing species such as *Salvia yangii* (syn. *Perovskia atriplicifolia*) and *Stipa gigantea* were planted as container stock. The first two years

required extensive weeding, allowing perennial seedlings to develop into larger plants and minimise competition. The result is a riot of colour and form with high species diversity. Some prominent species are *Rudbeckia fulgida*, *Silphium terebinthinaceum*, *Liatris pycnostachya*, *Eurybia spectabilis*, *Echinacea purpurea*, *Oenothera macrocarpa*, *Eryngium yuccifolium*, *Patrinia scabiosifolia*, *Aster amellus*, *Stipa gigantea*, *Hyssopus officinalis*, *Echinops ritro*, *Silphium laciniatum*, *Echinacea pallida* and *Salvia yangii* (syn. *Perovskia atriplicifolia*).

To create resilient, future-proof gardens that encourage wildlife, James stresses a high diversity of species is needed with intricate leaf, flower and stem structures. The benefit of creating plantings from seed is that seedlings develop and adapt to specific local soil and climatic conditions. Future seeds from these plants can develop more site-specific adaptations and be even better equipped to cope with changing local conditions.

KINGSWEAR GARDEN

Designers: Duncan Nuttall and AMELD

Location: Kingswear, Devon, England

Kingswear, a seaside village in Devon, south-west England, is known for its cliffs, beaches and mild maritime climate. Eight years ago, Duncan Nuttall, a garden maker living and working in south Devon, in collaboration with Devon-based AMELD (Artistically Made Ecological Landscape Design), designed major landscape interventions for a house and garden set on grey slate bluffs 15 m (50 ft) above the sea.

The house had a conventional garden with exotic species commonly planted on the English seaside, such as phormium and cordyline, but lacked visual affinity to the region.

Duncan removed concrete walls obstructing views and a length of tarmac drive to create a winding pedestrian path through planting to the front entrance. Cars are now parked uphill away from the house.

Stone from the house renovation that was initially quarried on site was kept and re-used to build dry stone walls that terrace the site's steep slope. Decking around the pool and on platforms near the water is made of oak timber sourced within 24 km (15 miles) of the property.

Planting for this exposed site was resilient, low maintenance and capable of dealing with salty winds. Duncan took clues from the landscape, using clipped shrubs to visually echo the cliffs and undulating sea. The side of the house facing the sea is richer in shrubs to create a shelterbelt, while a mass of floriferous herbaceous plants extends towards the pool area where conditions are more protected. Eryngium, ferula, althaea, nepeta, *Salvia yangii* (syn. *Perovskia atriplicifolia*), agapanthus, sedum and echium, among others, provide splashes of colour throughout the year.

This garden is guided rather than heavily managed, allowing self-seeding and weather to shape the planting. Soil depth was considered during construction to enable long-term success and allow plants to root in the underlying rocks for drought resistance. Seaweed collected from the beach is applied as fertiliser during autumn and winter.

Duncan has sensitively crafted minimal platforms for users to easily access the cliff face and shoreline below and enjoy the yellow-orange glow of *Caloplaca marina*, a sea lichen inhabiting the coastal rock surfaces in Devon.

WAKEHURST

Designers: Larry Weaner Landscape Associates (LWLA)

Location: Haywards Heath, West Sussex, England

Wakehurst (owned by the National Trust, and home to the Millennium Seed Bank) is used and managed by the Royal Botanic Gardens, Kew as a wild botanic garden. Here, with its new Landscape Ecology Programme, Wakehurst addresses the major environmental threats of biodiversity loss, climate change and land use change, advancing nature-based solutions and interventions in which humans act as 'ecological stewards of nature', recognising and valuing its benefits, and working with nature.

Famous for his meadow creations in the US, in 2019 Philadelphia-based Larry Weaner (LWLA) was approached by Wakehurst to bring North American prairies to the Sussex countryside.

In collaboration with Ed Ikin, Wakehurst's horticultural director, and landscape architects Land Use Consultants (LUC), Larry and his team analysed Wakehurst's climatic conditions to identify plant communities from three macro-regions in the US that best matched the south-east English climate: the Atlantic coastal plain prairie; the tall-grass prairie of the Midwest, and the Pacific Northwest prairie. In selecting species, Larry determined which could be seeded directly or introduced as potted specimens.

The Wakehurst team travelled to the US, hand-collecting millions of wild seeds from native prairies. Species they were unable to find were sourced through Prairie Moon Nursery in Minnesota. The seeds were mixed at the Millennium Seed Bank, with a selection kept in the nursery to germinate into 50,000 plug plants, each hand-planted a year later.

The prairie site was formerly a lawn with beds for shrubs, which meant soil conditions were different in composition and depth. Soil was mixed to create more homogeneous growing conditions and prevent plants from growing differently across the prairie. The area was seeded in 2019, planted in the autumn of 2020, and first came into flower in an impressive blanket of yellow in the summer of 2021.

The prairie is still in its juvenile stage, with short-lived perennials and biannuals like *Monarda citriodora* and *Rudbeckia hirta* visible in large numbers. These species will decrease gradually as the prairie matures and long-lived species become established. Short-lived species were mown in full bloom during the first summer, to allow long-lived resilient perennials such as *Baptisia* spp., liatris and veronicastrum to be planted. As the prairie develops, Wakehurst plans to introduce managed burning to maintain plant and animal diversity and remove dead vegetation.

A pioneering conservation landscape, Wakehurst's American Prairie also provides an attractive alternative to vast expanses of green lawn, increasingly unsustainable in the English climate. These photographs were taken in the summer of 2022, the warmest year on record, when heatwaves saw temperatures rise above +40 °C (104 °F) for the first time, and the UK received just 62 per cent of its annual summer rainfall.

MEADOW GARDEN

Designer: Jo McKerr

Location: Wellow, Somerset, England

Jo McKerr, a writer and garden designer, grew up in a dilapidated farmhouse on the edge of the Mendip Hills in Somerset. Twelve years ago, she moved with her family to a post-industrial brownfield site, in rolling countryside near Bath, complete with slurry yard, canal tunnel for the movement of coal, and a disused railway line.

Jo sensed the site's spirit of brutal wilderness and used it to preserve and guide her new interventions in the landscape. She was committed to maintaining the connection of the place to its rural context and industrial past. First, she observed the land around the house, conducted renovation work, and planted a mixed hedge and fruit trees. Broken-up concrete and rubble from the building renovation was recycled and used as fill material to create gentler slopes around the house.

Jo encourages biodiversity, restores habitats, and advances plant species adapted to their environment. No chemicals or fertilisers are used in the garden, and soil life is boosted using locally sourced woodchips, spread on the surface to help bring back mycorrhizal fungi into the degraded soil.

Sustainable design features include a pool fed by recycled rainwater, a drought-tolerant gravel garden, and a native wildflower meadow. The garden is not irrigated. With increasingly record-breaking summer temperatures, Jo advocates for a new garden aesthetic in the UK.

KITCHEN GARDEN AT RHS GARDEN BRIDGEWATER

Designer: Charlotte Harris and Hugo Bugg of Harris Bugg Studio

Location: Salford, Manchester, England

Addressing what we eat and how we produce our food plays a key role in dealing with climate change. This is where the New Kitchen Garden comes into play at RHS Bridgewater, an inspirational setting for highlighting the importance of our food choices and how they impact our carbon footprint.

The UK's fifth Royal Horticultural Society public garden opened in 2021 in Salford, a metropolitan borough within Greater Manchester. The RHS invited Charlotte Harris and Hugo Bugg, now RHS Chelsea Flower Show Best in Show winners, to design an evolving kitchen garden.

The design of the garden's main pathways is inspired by the route of the adjacent Bridgewater Canal, and minor pathways found on historic maps from the late 19th century. Vegetable cultivation is celebrated, as well as local heritage and craftsmanship. Four distinct zones include an edible forest garden, formal kitchen garden, modern apothecary and edimental garden and fruit-training garden. To retain its vernacular identity, wall copings were constructed in local stone, and onsite architectural elements influenced the design of seven towers for unusual edible climbers.

Sustainable practices include biological pest control, permaculture principles, seasonal food production, no-dig techniques, water-saving methods and pollinator-friendly edible plants.

Sharing the vast selection of plants that can now be grown because of climate change (even in northern England), the RHS Garden Bridgewater is actively encouraging and educating people to grow pollinator-friendly plants, try companion planting and find inspiration for their vegetable plots.

AUSTRALIAN GARDENS

Designers: Phillip Johnson Landscapes
Location: Euroa and Olinda, Victoria, Australia

Australian garden designer Phillip Johnson, and his highly qualified team at Phillip Johnson Landscapes, design, build and maintain sustainable habitats that help to heal the earth and renew an appreciation for nature. For more than two decades Phillip Johnson has led the way in sustainable landscape design, working to overcome the demands of increasing water restrictions and climatic changes, and celebrating Australia's natural beauty. Phillip was awarded Gold and Best in Show at the 2013 RHS Chelsea Flower Show – a first for an Australian team.

EUROA

Eddie and Dot Spain's house (featured on the TV series *Grand Designs Australia*) sits on 40 ha (98 acres) in Victoria's Strathbogie Ranges – a dry, windy location with considerable temperature fluctuations.

Phillip reclaimed rocks removed during building works, placing them close to the house, while a native plant palette responds to rocky terrain: *Xanthorrhoea glauca* (grass tree), *Xerochrysum bracteatum* and *Chrysocephalum apiculatum* (everlasting daisies), *Grevillea excelsior* and *Eucalyptus pauciflora* (snow gum). A remnant eucalyptus trunk was left in place as both a sculpture and a subtle reminder of the fragility of nature.

All planted areas are lightly mounded and mulched with local crushed granite gravel, a fireproof material which also acts to prevent erosion, maintain moisture, and regulate the soil temperature in all seasons. Plants are irrigated on establishment only, and are required to survive fire and thrive without water.

CHELSEA AUSTRALIAN GARDEN AT OLINDA

Ten years after winning Gold and Best in Show at the prestigious Royal Horticultural Society (RHS) Chelsea Flower Show, Phillip Johnson re-created his award-winning Australian Garden in the Dandenong Ranges Botanic Garden in Olinda. The new garden (jointly funded by state and federal governments and the People and Parks Foundation) is over 20 times the size of the original Chelsea Flower Show build and converts a section of the former Olinda Golf Course into a stunning botanic garden, supporting biodiversity and habitat creation.

It is a real homecoming for the garden – Phillip was originally inspired to create the Australian Garden by 'Billabong Falls', his own Olinda garden in the Dandenong Ranges.

The Chelsea Australian Garden – off grid with no reliance on mains power or water – showcases sustainable and waterwise design, including an integrated bushfire protection system, solar power and the clever use of recycled and reclaimed materials (e.g. seating crafted from the Dandenong Ranges storm recovery program). It features 15,000 plants from over 400 native Australian species and includes rare and endangered species such as the Wollemi pine.

The Phillip Johnson team excels at bringing spaces to life that astound people, connecting them to nature and Country, while also allowing native birds, bees and other pollinators to thrive. A cascading waterfall (recirculated using solar/battery power), a rocky gorge and billabong provide new homes for local frogs. Stormwater runoff is captured to store and clean over one million litres of water, and to slow down the storm surge. This in turn prevents erosion and damage to natural creeks and gullies downstream.

In June 2023, Phillip told attendees at the official opening, 'I hope visitors feel a sense of awe when they visit the garden, and I hope they leave feeling inspired to protect Australia's special landscapes – and maybe even create something new in their own garden.'

MORNINGTON GARDEN

Designers: Jane Jones Landscapes
Location: Mornington, Victoria, Australia

Coastal vibes feature in this Mornington garden south-east of Melbourne where local garden designer Jane Jones was asked to renovate an old garden overwhelmed by weeds. The Mornington Peninsula, known for its scenic landscape, sandy beaches and wineries, has a mild, oceanic climate with warm summers and cool winters.

Jane's design was shaped by the site, on a clifftop facing Port Phillip Bay with big sky views. The garden, on sloping ground above the house and adjacent to a golf course, is exposed to salty winds, and site access was difficult.

Crowded and overgrown plants were removed, replaced by a mixture of robust, drought-resistant, native and non-native species. Resilient genera added throughout the property include eryngium, teucrium, dymondia, elaeagnus, pittosporum, casuarina, agastache, banksia and westringia. For movement, Jane incorporated ornamental grasses, such as miscanthus, panicum and lomandra. Yellow-flowering native *Pycnosorus globosu*s (or Billy buttons) provides pleasing contrast against the expanse of blue sky.

The garden is minimally irrigated, with two small lawn areas forming a negative space among generously planted beds.

While Jane puts successful planting down to choices made for coastal conditions, she acknowledges that long-term success and design integrity rely on good maintenance.

WILDCOAST

Designer: Sam Cox
Location: Portsea, Victoria, Australia

Wildcoast's garden, embedded in a coastal dune landscape on the edge of Point Nepean National Park, was created by Melbourne-based landscape designer Sam Cox, around a wood-clad cantilevered house by Sean Godsell Architects.

Sam has designed and built gardens since 1999, reinterpreting an Australian natural style developed by local garden makers Edna Walling, Ellis Stones and Gordon Ford. Ford's five-decade garden design legacy profoundly influenced Sam's passion for naturalistic design, using Australian native plants to create gardens with non-defined boundaries.

Inspiration came from existing plants: soft, green-grey tones of the indigenous vegetation. Once the house construction was completed, Sam worked to heal and revegetate the land, modelling the dunes around the house, working within surrounding contours. No walls or steps were constructed.

Before any new planting, the invasive South African *Polygala myrtifolia*, was removed. Approximately 2,500 endemic plants, including *Leptospermum laevigatum*, *Melaleuca lanceolata*, *Banksia integrifolia* and several local wattle species, were introduced to the site.

Plantings were mulched with a 10 cm (4 in) layer of recycled timber chippings, also used for covering dune pathways that connect the house to discreet, carved-out places: a fire pit, trampoline and camping areas.

In Wildcoast, Sam continues Gordon Ford's design legacy, celebrating the blurred lines between wild and cultivated (mass and void).

THE FAMILY GARDEN

Designer: Jo Ferguson
Location: Flinders, Victoria, Australia

Jo studied native grasslands at Burnley Gardens, part of the University of Melbourne's School of Agriculture, and has a passion for engaging with stories revealed in gardens and landscape – their family garden is situated on the ancient lands of the Boonwurrung people.

Before starting their family garden, Jo and her husband Simon Hazel considered what brought them most joy in a garden. For Simon, it was memories of observing insect activity and growing vegetables. For Jo, it was being immersed in nature, particularly native grasses. They agreed their garden should combine all elements; the feel more important than how it looked.

The Mornington Peninsula is on volcanic country and has a mild oceanic climate, cool winters, and clay soil with superb water retention (irrigation is rarely needed).

Jo and Simon planted native and exotic species selected 'for love' rather than a defined style or theme. Trees planted were chosen for their grey-blue foliage to ground the garden in its native landscape and create a strong sense of place. Resilient species were selected to tolerate a wide range of environmental conditions without the need for continuous attention.

Prominent native Australian species used include *Eucalyptus latens* 'Moon Lagoon', *Austrostipa verticillata* (slender bamboo grass), *Austrostipa stipoides* (coastal spear grass), *Themeda triandra* (kangaroo grass), *Correa alba* (white correa), *Banksia drummondii* and paper daisies *Xerochrysum bracteatum* 'Lemon Monarch' and 'Strawberry Blonde' intermingled with *Dichelachne crinita* (longhair plume grass).

For Jo, the garden is a source of joy and connection – a fantasy grassland matrix composed of tall native and exotic grasses interspersed with perennials and native shrubs for structure and year-round presence. The composition of plants could only work here, in an Australian naturalistic style defined by a bushland character with numerous species intermingled, allowed to self-seed and colonise bare ground.

MELBOURNE CITY GARDEN

Designers: Amanda Oliver Gardens
Location: Melbourne, Victoria, Australia

This small urban garden, on a sunny, north-facing slope in the Melbourne suburb of Kew, is where landscape designer Amanda Oliver created a plant-driven garden, tying a modern brutalist house (by local architect Paul Couch) to the landscape.

In the front garden, local indigenous grasses and copses of *Corymbia citriodora* (dwarf lemon scented gums) line the driveway. In the back garden, a swimming pool is completely enveloped by plants growing up to the water. Planting features drought-tolerant native and non-native perennials, grasses and succulents, featuring a sophisticated, cool-coloured composition of leaf shapes and textures rather than flowers. A drip irrigation system keeps plants lush during severe drought, lowering the air temperature through evapotranspiration.

The entire garden is free draining. Rather than formal paths, bluestone stepping stones with less planting in the gravel areas delineate a way to move through the garden.

TRENTHAM GARDEN

Designer: Simon Rickard

Location: Trentham, Victoria, Australia

Trentham lies on a tableland 700 m (2,300 ft) above sea level, north-west of Melbourne where the climate has more in common with the Pacific Coast Ranges, Chilean Andes, and north-western Spain, than it does with most parts of Australia. It features a short growing season and relatively high annual rainfall, compared with Melbourne's noticeably warmer, drier climate.

Even this relatively mild climate has changed in the 18 years that Simon has gardened there – the difference between 'hot, dry years' and 'cold, wet years' has become ever more pronounced. Simon observes, 'there is simultaneously not enough heat

to grow tomatoes, but more heat than "English" plants can tolerate – a challenge, but with the right plants, gardening is possible in any climate.'

Simon is frustrated by what he sees as a puritanical streak existing in Australian horticulture, whereby Australian native plants are seen as the only 'moral' choice, and the inclusion of exotic plants is viewed as environmental vandalism. Yet a plant from the mountains of South Africa, or the foothills of the Andes, can be a better match for Simon's climate than one from Sydney or Brisbane.

Using this approach to plant selection, Simon creates exuberant, challenging compositions which don't exist in nature. His front garden is based on textures and architectural foliage. In summer, a meadow-style 'privy garden' flourishes with grasses and perennials. An explosion of autumn colour heralds peak season in his woodland garden, giving way to winter flowering bulbs, evergreen foliage, and winter twigs and barks. This joyful, species-rich garden hums with wildlife.

GARDEN FOR THE FUTURE

Designers: T.C.L (Taylor Cullity Lethlean) / Paul Thompson

Location: Bendigo, Victoria, Australia

One of Victoria's oldest botanic gardens – founded in 1857 – is also one of its most futuristic. In 2018 the 'Garden for the Future', a new 3.5 ha (8.6 acre) extension to the historic White Hills Botanic Gardens, opened as the first built phase of a master plan for the regional city of Bendigo.

Taylor Cullity Lethlean (TCL), worked with acclaimed Australian landscape horticulturist Paul Thompson, to choose a palette of species to thrive in extreme current and forecasted climatic conditions. Global environments with temperatures and rainfall like those predicted for Bendigo over the next 50 years were analysed and used as a guide for plant selection.

Features include a central event lawn and amphitheatre space – the Fun and Fantasy Lawn – framed by richly planted beds, with views to a small stage and shelter area. An oval-shaped promenade wraps around the lawn. Extensive display gardens are divided into native and exotic plantings. The exotic species are chosen from areas around the world with similar climatic conditions including South America, the African continent and Mediterranean region with a focus on resilience, robustness, adaptability and display.

Bendigo Creek flows parallel to the botanic garden, posing an inundation risk as unpredictable weather patterns intensify. As part of the design, the central lawn acts as a detention basin for diverted rainwater during significant rain events. Plants are irrigated with recycled water during establishment, adapting the garden to future water restrictions and prolonged drought. Hard landscape materials were sourced locally, reducing transport and minimising the carbon footprint.

This new botanic garden, designed for a rapidly changing climate, not only ensures the garden's survival, but educates and inspires visitors to see how climate-appropriate plants can be used in new and interesting ways. The Garden for the Future is a testing ground for all of us.

GLENLUCE GARDEN

Designers: Michael Wright and Catherine Rush (Rush Wright Associates)

Location: Glenluce, Victoria, Australia

Catherine Rush and Michael Wright are founding directors of Melbourne-based landscape architecture firm Rush Wright Associates. Each with over 30 years of experience in the field, they lead a team of 15 landscape architects. Their weekend home in Glenluce, north-west of Melbourne, experiences extreme climatic conditions: hot summers, prolonged droughts, and regular bushfires.

In front of the tiny west-facing house, helped by their friend, fellow landscape architect Thomas Gooch, they created and built a garden inspired by the wind-shaped dunes of Wyperfeld National Park, western Victoria. Finger-shaped, slightly mounded planting areas, reminiscent of the dunes, are interspersed with elongated, sand-covered paths.

A generous stone fire-pit area – the garden's focal point, built with local rocks – is positioned to make the most of stunning views of the surrounding area, and, on a clear night, a vast, star-filled sky.

The whole garden is like a giant creek bed capable of acting as a reservoir, covered with a layer of 10 cm (4 in) of sand, below which there is a geotextile (permeable fabric), and 20 cm (8 in) of gravel under the paths. Underlying clay soil prevents rapid water infiltration and forms a perfect base for containing stormwater. Buff sand mimics the tones of dry grass covering the paddocks around the property, visually blending the garden with its surroundings, particularly in summer.

Fire retardant plants such as *Atriplex nummularia* (Australian saltbush) create a native, fire protective buffer between the garden and adjacent paddock, along with the iconic grass tree, *Xanthorrhoea* 'Supergrass' a hybrid cross between *X. johnsonii* and *X. glauca*. *Xerochrysum bracteatum* (native drought-tolerant strawflowers, or paper daisies) provide colourful accents for months and self-seed freely. Resilient exotic species from the Mediterranean and US arid regions are planted closer to the house.

Michael and Catherine have created a low-budget garden that incorporates smart strategies for long-term success in a challenging, fire-prone environment. It also recreates the wow factor of the Australian bush in a small, designed space.

YALAMURRA

Designer: Kurt Wilkinson

Location: Adelaide Hills, South Australia, Australia

In a rugged, dry and hilly landscape an hour north-east of Adelaide, professional gardener and topiarist Kurt Wilkinson has created a colourful ornamental landscape around his home garden Yalamurra.

The self-taught gardener working in the Adelaide area mainly tended traditional urban plots with irrigated lawns, borders and hedges, and only recently started designing gardens by introducing waterwise practices and species into his clients' gardens. Kurt references the work of Piet Oudolf and *Dreamscapes* (Hardie Grant, 2018) as significant recent inspirations, opening his eyes to the world of naturalistic planting – surprising, given that he has only visited the gardens in which he works.

His 3 ha (11 acre) hilltop site is challenging, characterised by a harsh climate with little summer rain and low air moisture over warmer months. Initially, Kurt failed to grasp the complexities of gardening in such an exposed rocky area. Nor did he appreciate the environmental hurdles of growing plants outside their natural range. He tried seeding and growing perennials and grasses featured in notable projects by Piet Oudolf, Nigel Dunnett and James Hitchmough. Despite extensive effort and irrigation to keep plants growing, all failed. Kurt subsequently discovered that the soil on his property has the water mould *Phytophthora*, one of the reasons why many plants collapsed even when they were watered.

After many failures, Kurt was forced to rethink his planting strategy; necessity required him to diversify his tastes. He started trialling succulents, looking at the roadside for inspiration, and learning about species that were fully self-sustaining.

Using plants thriving in the area and ceasing irrigating were turning points for Kurt's garden philosophy.

The garden is now wild and vibrant. Eye-catching plant groupings juxtapose with formal clipped elements, such as carefully pruned *Cupressus sempervirens*, with informal natural forms and messy randomised vegetation. Robust species include *Aeonium arboreum*, *Centaurea gymnocarpa*, *Lavandula dentata*, *Melaleuca nesophila*, *Alyogyne huegelii*, leucadendron, aloe and agapanthus.

To keep the xeric species happy, Kurt makes the growing conditions even more extreme, encouraging long life with little attention. The garden is constantly regenerated by allowing self-sowing and cuttings.

Yalamurra is a meaningful step toward a sustainable future in garden making, a beautiful example of how we can improve our gardens rather than simply help them to survive.

BARANGAROO

**Designers: Peter Walker and David Walker,
PWP Landscape Architecture / Johnson Pilton
Walker (JPW)**
Location: Sydney, New South Wales, Australia

Before colonisation, this headland was a rolling wooded landscape used for fishing and hunting by the Gadigal people of the Eora Nation, traditional custodians of the Sydney region. The natural landscape was entirely erased during the 19th and 20th centuries to make way for wharves and piers. The 6 ha (15 acre) foreshore park and cultural facility (opened in 2015 south of Sydney Harbour Bridge) was named after Barangaroo, a Cammeraygal clan woman and powerful indigenous voice during the colonisation of New South Wales.

US-based PWP Landscape Architecture and Sydney-based Johnson Pilton Walker (JPW) worked in collaboration to recreate an idealised version of the pre-1836 shoreline topography and landscape. The reserve incorporates a sustainability commitment to creating a carbon neutral district following the One Planet Sustainable Programme.

Parkland features lawns, cycle and walking paths, lookouts, two new coves, extensive planting areas and a new rocky shoreline with tidal pools. Most of the 10,000 Hawkesbury sandstone blocks used to edge the re-imagined foreshore were extracted directly from the site. Asphalt from the former harbour area was recycled and used as a road base, and all the loose material excavated from the coves were used as fill below the headland.

Under the guidance of soil scientists, soils excavated around the site were repurposed to create a shallow, free-draining topsoil. Large stormwater tanks were installed for irrigation, and LED lighting and solar panels were used across the park.

All plant species used in Barangaroo are native, most of them to Sydney Harbour. Planting included 75,000 trees and shrubs. Local horticulturist Stuart Pittendrigh (a fellow of the Australian Institute of Horticulture) worked closely with PWP Landscape Architecture to select resilient, drought-tolerant species capable of withstanding current and future unstable climatic conditions.

Woody and herbaceous species used throughout the park include *Allocasurina littoralis* (black she-oak), *Angophora costata* (Sydney red gum), *Banksia integrifolia* (coast banksia), *Corymbia gummifera* (red bloodwood), *Austrodanthonia richardsonii* (wallaby grass), *Dianella caerulea* (blue flax lily), *Acacia longifolia* (Sydney golden wattle), *Westringia fruticosa* (coastal rosemary), *Xanthorrhoea media* (grass tree) and *Lomandra longifolia* (mat rush). Most of the species have significant cultural uses for the indigenous community.

Barangaroo sets high sustainability and place-making standards for public open spaces. Using 100 per cent recycled materials, native resilient plant species and net positive water use, it is an outstanding symbol of reconciliation with its First Nations past.

SYDNEY METRO PLANTING TRIAL

Designer: Jon Hazelwood (Hassell), John Rayner and Claire Farrell (University of Melbourne)

Location: Sydney, New South Wales, Australia

The busy Hills Showground Station Plaza in suburban Castle Hill is an unexpected location for a visionary plant trial, a design collaboration between NSW government transport agency Sydney Metro, Professors Claire Farrell and John Rayner from the University of Melbourne, and Jon Hazelwood from Hassell architects.

In the trial, launched in 2022, plant behaviour and evolution are closely monitored to identify the most robust species and plant mixes for a 'Nature Positive City'. Planting is photographed every two weeks with changes recorded. Planting comprises approximately 100 herbaceous, predominantly native species, grouped and arranged in a naturalistic, randomised layout combined with coppiced shrubs. Species are planted in free-draining roof soil medium at various densities.

Weeding, watering and plant replacements are significantly reduced by using a novel, low-cost resilient alternative to conventional plantings. The trial aims to increase biodiversity in cities, creating a more lively and attractive public landscape.

SPRING BAY MILL

Designer: Marcus Ragus (Verdant Way)
Location: Triabunna, Tasmania, Australia

Spring Bay Mill occupies a native forest and grassland peninsula on Freestone Point, Triabunna. This was once a Tasmanian Aboriginal gathering place for Palawa people. The world's largest woodchip mill was sited here from the 1970s to its closure in 2011 when environmentalist Graeme Wood purchased the mill to restore the landscape's ecology.

The industrial site on 42 ha (100 acres) of land was rejuvenated by recycling buildings and artefacts into a sustainable events venue, restaurant, conference centre and accommodation facilities.

Marcus Ragus, a Tasmanian landscape designer and horticulturist, was brought on board to re-imagine the site, and lead remediation and restoration of the contaminated ecosystem. A guiding concept was to create a resilient and attractive landscape using native plants that grow within 50 km (30 miles) of the site.

The site was challenging, with large expanses of concrete and bitumen as well as onsite industrial materials, many of which were re-used. For example, a large section of the site, the former woodchip storage area, was repurposed in collaboration with architect Ross Brewin, into an amphitheatre and native dune grassland landscape. Additionally, the original weighbridge building was deconstructed and made into a gazebo-like 'garden folly', covered with a local native climber, the purple apple berry, *Billardiera longiflora*.

Over 20,000 endemic species were planted. An onsite nursery produces approximately 10,000 plants annually, reintroducing native grasses and other species that existed prior to European settlement, such as *Poa labillardierei*, *Banksia marginata*, *Lomandra longifolia*, *Eucalyptus globulus* and *E. viminalis*. The site welcomed back native wildlife, including possums, wombats, echidnas, tiger and copperhead snakes, and many bird species.

The landscape design on the large amphitheatre site includes the windswept 'Aeolean mounds'. These fluid, crescent-headed dunes are planted out with native grasses, and mulched with locally sourced dolerite rock gravel that acknowledges natural dune shapes in the landscape. They also provide visitors with some protection from the elements.

Controlled burning of natural bushland was reintroduced with indigenous rangers to educate visitors about ancient land management practices while also improving the native plant and animal diversity of the area. The new plant landscapes are now virtually self-sustaining, being ideally adapted to meeting the climate and extremes of the area. Rainwater storage tanks provide water for irrigation, drinking and sanitation, while solar panels provide energy for accommodation cabins in a model for environmentally neutral events venues in a post-industrial site.

Graeme and his partner Anna Cerneaz's vision for people gathering on the site, just as Aboriginal people had done in the past, has been successfully achieved at Spring Bay Mill – proof that in regenerating landscapes, we regenerate ourselves.

TASMANIAN COASTAL LANDSCAPE

Designers: Jennie and Rob Churchill
Location: Dolphin Sands, Tasmania, Australia

The Churchills, both retired veterinarians, are life-long advocates for plants and the environment. Kiloren, their previous garden in New South Wales, was designed by Australian landscape designer Edna Walling, and was a cool-climate garden of water-hungry European species. Jennie and Rob realised they wanted a different kind of garden – self-sufficient and in tune with the landscape.

In 2005, they purchased 2 ha (5 acres) at Dolphin Sands on Tasmania's east coast, with iconic views of Freycinet National Park. The sand dune plot was vegetated with *Banksia marginata* and *Acacia longifolia* ssp. *sophorae,* the ground cover dominated by invasive *Ammophila arenaria* (European marram grass). In 2009, a devastating bushfire destroyed all original vegetation. From the following autumn, Jennie and Rob have revegetated with over 20,000 plants, using native east coast species including *Poa poiformis* (coastal tussock grass), *Ficinia nodosa* (knobby club-rush), *Correa alba* (white correa), and fire-resistant native pigface (carpobrotus) and salt bush (rhagodia).

Instead of a garden, Jennie refers to 'habitat for wildlife'. Embedded in the dunes as part of the landscape, the house is surrounded by a network of pathways and selected plants are allowed to grow right up to it. Burnt timbers are left standing as perching habitat for birds or levelled on the ground as rotting habitat and refuge for smaller species.

Invasive marram grass continues to be removed from large areas around the house. Pulled by hand, it is an ongoing and relentless task. Otherwise, land is lightly managed: monitoring marram regrowth, maintaining paths and clearings, keeping the coastal wattle in check and utilising its debris as a natural mulch for pathways.

The greatest joy for Jennie and Rob is in seeing wildlife respond to their efforts. From her office window, Jennie watches fairy wrens, fantails, honeyeaters, and black cockatoos feeding on banksia seed heads, while lizards, echidnas and red-necked wallabies have all returned.

AMONG TALL TREES

Designers: Mark and Keryn Fountain

Location: Mount Rumney, Tasmania, Australia

With their highly compatible creative passions, garden designer Mark Fountain and his partner, artist Keryn Fountain, have crafted a garden within a eucalyptus forest on a dry, sunny slope in Mount Rumney, 12 km (7.5 miles) from Tasmania's capital, Hobart.

Mark, a former deputy director of the Royal Tasmanian Botanical Gardens in Hobart, has designed with and grown plants since his early twenties, while Keryn's source of inspiration as an artist is how humans see patterns and signs in nature.

The house was built in 1958 in the mid-century modern style, influenced in part by both the Bauhaus

movement and Japanese architecture and design. Inspired by their own travels in Japan, the garden needed to complement the modernist building's style and context.

Using a deliberately limited palette of mostly drought-tolerant Tasmanian species, Mark and Keryn have created a loose, naturalistic garden that gently flows into the landscape, characterised by three native Eucalyptus species (*Eucalyptus viminalis*, *E. pulchella* and *E. globulus*) that form a grove around the house with attractive, dappled shade. A significant number of plants, including *Clematis gentianoides*, *Brachyscome* and *Wahlenbergia* spp. were propagated from seed collected on the hillside.

Ground covers including *Myoporum parvifolium* and the Tasmanian endemic *Lasiopetalum micranthum* are used to visually simplify and give shape to the garden. The myoporum provides a rich green in even the driest years.

Experimental ornamental plantings include a delicate mixture of Tasmanian herbaceous perennials and grasses used in generous blocks. The garden has a peak moment from spring to mid-summer and slows down during drought. Planting areas are not regularly watered, although three rainwater tanks provide occasional irrigation. Stone used for paving is collected on site, with concrete steps tying the garden to the architecture of the house.

Although purposely designed and constructed by Mark and Keryn, being in the garden feels like being in the wild. Sustainable design embraces site challenges, finding materiality and planting strategies to create a place with a sophisticated personality that is also very Tasmanian.

MT PISA GARDEN

Designer: Jo Wakelin

Location: Mt Pisa, Central Otago, New Zealand

This stunning, intentionally humble and simple garden sits at the foot of the Pisa Range in Central Otago, the driest and coldest area of New Zealand.

Jo Wakelin, a trained ecologist and horticulture lecturer, wanted the garden to have the feel of a 'distilled droplet' at the base of a crucible reflecting and seamlessly connecting to the colours and shapes of the surrounding mountain ranges. Two 'tear drops' symbolise the preciousness of water and a sense of 'duality' is created: native plants versus exotic; water versus dry; stone tear drop versus planted tear drop.

It is hard to believe this landscape was barren 18 years ago when the house was built – the natural vegetation denuded by rabbits and sheep. While looking to the future, Jo's garden design also references the region's glacial origins and mining history from the 1860s gold-rush period.

From a planting perspective, the garden is divided into two halves: the exotic section to the side of the house with xeric species from the US, the Mediterranean and Asia, which have similar climates; and New Zealand natives at the front of the house, overlooking the pond. Much of the biodiversity explosion is a result of the pond and starkly contrasting garden, with dry stony habitat for native lizards and many different bees (including native) flourishing amongst the plantings. Jo prefers drought-loving rather than drought-resistant species for their ability to thrive in dry, free-draining substrates rather than merely survive.

Poa cita, a native silver tussock, creates a mini-meadow with characteristic brown-yellow colours connecting to tones of the mountain slopes. Endemic species *Carex secta* and *C. virgata* grow around the pond. Non-native species include *Iris barbata*, *Tanacetum* spp., *Phlomis italica*, *P. fruticosa*, *P. purpurea*, *P. lanata*, *Salvia argentea*, *Rosa rugosa*, *Centranthus ruber*, *Elaeagnus* 'Quicksilver', *Dianthus deltoides*, *Ballota pseudodictamnus*, *Euphorbia rigida*, *E. spinosa*, *Asphodeline lutea* and yucca, *Salvia yangii*, verbascum and santolina species.

Pea gravel, a waste product from a local quarry, covers the ground throughout and materials such as salvaged timber bridge piles have been repurposed as vertical man-made elements, juxtaposed against the planting. A pond built close to the house hosts frogs and attracts many species of native birds. For Jo, relying on rainfall for plant survival promotes better connection with both environment and climate. Her garden excels at making minimal demands on resources.

GREENING OF SINGAPORE

Singapore's status as one of the greenest cities in the world, and most sustainable cities in Asia, began in the 1960s. What began as an aesthetic and cultural consideration, with extensive tree planting along boulevards, led to widespread creation of parks, park connectors, green corridors and nature reserves. Currently more than half of Singapore's land is covered in green spaces. Today, the city's impressive greening policy is evolving further as it transforms from a 'City in a Garden' to a 'City in Nature'. This is a key pillar of the Green Plan 2030, where scientific and functional values are connected to create a more liveable, biodiverse, sustainable and climate-resilient nation.

The government launched the Green Plan in 2021, encouraging citizen involvement in the transformation. Initiatives include setting aside 50 per cent more land for nature parks; planting one million more trees; and an additional 1,000 ha (2,500 acres) of green spaces.

GARDENS BY THE BAY

One of Singapore's more famed attractions, Gardens by the Bay is a centrally located 101 ha (250 acre) nature park and botanic garden. The gardens showcase the plant kingdom in an immersive and engaging way, while implementing sustainable cycles in energy and water.

The park comprises three distinctive waterfront gardens: Bay South, Bay East and Bay Central. Bay South with its cooled conservatories and iconic 50 m (165 ft) high 'Supertree' structures (designed by UK-based Grant Associates), harvest solar energy on their canopies for lighting.

Several hundred mangrove trees within the Dragonfly Lakes and Kingfisher Wetlands function as a carbon sink by removing greenhouse gases from the environment. *See pages 204-207.*

BISHAN-ANG MO KIO PARK

One of Singapore's most popular heartland parks, defined by the meandering Kallang River, is a flagship project of the Active, Beautiful, Clean Waters (ABC Waters) Programme, launched in 2006 to clean and rejuvenate the country's rivers and lakes.

In 2007, the Public Utilities Board and National Parks Board of Singapore appointed German-based Studio Dreiseitl to naturalise and integrate the park's old concrete canal into a natural river landscape – a first for Singapore – allowing visitors to reconnect with water and wildlife. The whole 62 ha (153 acre) urban park was redesigned to accommodate seasonal river water fluctuation, lowering the risk of flooding. Plants, rocks and bio-engineering techniques soften the waterway edges of this visionary project. *See page 208 Bishan-Ang Mo Kio Park (top), Singapore Botanic Gardens green roof (bottom).*

SINGAPORE CITY BUILDINGS

Nature is consciously woven throughout the city, especially in new building developments where plants occupy green roofs, vertical gardens and walls. *Buildings shown on this page include Parkroyal Collection Pickering (above left) and Oasis Hotel (above right).*

NATIONAL UNIVERSITY OF SINGAPORE

Since the 1960s the majority of Singapore's green spaces were modelled on English parkland, with highly manicured vegetation. A shift in aesthetics has occured in the past decade, helped largely by the studies and work of Associate Professor Yun Hye Hwang, a landscape architect and director of the National University of Singapore's Bachelor of Landscape Architecture programme. Hwang spent 15 years studying the potential of 'Intended Wildness' in Singapore, and conducted studies (e.g. 'It's OK to be Wilder') which show the public now accept moderately wilder, urban greenery, providing 'cues to care'.

Hwang explains the ecological benefits of more complex landscapes (as opposed to heavily maintained gardens) are nutrient accumulation in soil, prevention of erosion, heat mitigation, and habitat for wildlife.

At NUS, Hwang has introduced multi-layered, highly biodiverse plantings amongst the university campus, as well as edge treatments to lawn areas, surrounding multifunctional test plots of longer grass areas where edible plants are incorporated. Green corridors connect buildings, walkways and surroundings. *See pages 210-211*

MARINA ONE

Designers: Gustafson Porter + Bowman

Marina One is an innovative, sustainable, high-density building complex built on reclaimed land along the city's waterfront in Singapore's Marina Bay Financial District. It comprises four towers designed by Ingenhoven Architects arranged around a lush courtyard, the 'Green Heart' conceived by Gustafson Porter + Bowman.

The multipurpose public garden, developed in collaboration with ICN Design International, resembles a gradated forest. Planting along the building's elevation simulates rainforest valley vegetation that changes with altitude: 'Green Heart' at the lower level, 'Cloud Forest' in the middle, and 'Mountain Peak' at the top of the towers.

This project meets the LEED (Leadership in Energy and Environmental Design) Platinum pre-certification for sustainable design and is an excellent example of the seamless integration between landscape and architecture in a tropical climate.

KHOO TECK PUAT HOSPITAL

Designers: CPG Consultants

The Khoo Teck Puat Hospital, which opened in 2010, won the inaugural Stephen R. Kellert Biophilic Design Award. CPG Consultants designed the building to create a calm, relaxing environment, integrating nature wherever possible.

The building has a V-shape, with a central green court opening to the north, embracing the lushness of the adjacent Yishun stormwater pond. Design channels the prevailing north-east winds, providing a cooling effect and reducing energy consumption, lowering the hospital's reliance on mechanical ventilation by 60 per cent. The façade aluminium fins direct the wind while allowing patients views of the vegetation and access to natural light without the interference of solar glare or rain.

Water features, waterfalls and plants provide habitat for butterflies and birds, with over 90 different species. Indigenous tropical vegetation extends from a central courtyard to the upper levels, making the hospital feel entirely embedded in the garden. This project achieved a GPR (Green Plot Ratio) of 3.92, whereby the total vegetation area (vertical and horizontal) is almost four times the size of the hospital plot. On the rooftop, an abundant vegetable garden run by volunteers provides fresh produce for patients. Other gardens are scattered across the complex, allowing patients and staff to access green spaces easily.

COLESON BRUCE GARDEN

Designers: Coleson Bruce and John Ignacio
Location: Austin, Texas, USA

Interest in gardening and nature has been unprecedented since the COVID pandemic, and many people with little or no time for gardening were inspired to grow plants and experience the mental health benefits of green spaces.

This dry crevice garden, atypical to Austin suburbs, resulted from a collaboration during the summer of 2020 between its owner Coleson Bruce, a lawyer with a young family, and his friend and neighbour John Ignacio, a gardener and plantsman.

The mid-century single-storey house sits on the ridge above Bull Creek in north-west Austin, with direct views across the creek to tall limestone bluffs. The building's façade is covered with rounded, local limestone rocks, which visually connect the house with the broader landscape.

Coleson drew inspiration for the garden from an interest in sculpture and his experience as a park ranger in the mountain ranges of the Mojave desert in California, where he observed beauty in arid vegetation. A Texas-adapted crevice garden was created in front of the house, previously occupied by conventional lawn with junipers. The plants chosen are robust species of succulents, cacti, palms and perennials that thrive in Austin's hot and humid subtropical climate without significant irrigation. The garden emerged over six months from John's deep knowledge of plants and Coleson's artistic eye for composition and form.

The crevice garden between the circular drive and street features slabs of limestone laid on the side, and small rocks with gravel filling gaps. Most species in this area are high desert plants that can withstand occasional cold snaps and very high temperatures. *Echinocereus*, *Agave parryi*, *Hamelia patens*, *Cylindropuntia leptocaulis* and several palms are more prominent members of this dry plant community.

Another garden frames the house and the red entrance door on the other side of the drive. Here drought-tolerant species include *Yucca rostrata*, prostrate rosemary, *Hesperaloe campanulata*, *Serenoa repens*, lantana, salvia and a rare ocotillo, planted among limestone boulders. Apart from occasional weed removal, planting areas require little maintenance, mulched with decomposed granite gravel which keeps the soil moist.

This garden challenges the conventional aesthetic of suburban front yards in Austin, typically disconnected from the region's natural environment. It also embodies a beautiful story of collaboration and mutual effort between two friends during difficult times.

PERALTA LANE GARDEN

Designer: Amy Hovis (Eden Garden Design)
Location: Austin, Texas, USA

Karen and Stuart Goodman's house is in a new neighbourhood development in west Austin where landscape design is often dominated by large areas of irrigated lawns, flower beds sparsely planted and covered with bark mulch, and abundant use of river rocks to conceal any remaining open ground. With concerns about the increasing price of water, Karen and Stuart took a bold step to transform their backyard, opting for a sustainable and waterwise landscape, more in tune with the surrounding native vegetation.

Since 2013, Amy Hovis and her team at Eden have created natural retreats in mostly urban settings, with designed spaces that bring people and plants together. Here, they suggested reducing the amount of irrigated lawn and dividing the backyard into two zones with a steel retaining wall to accommodate the sloping terrain. The upper zone close to the house retains a formal character with a flat, infinity edge lawn. The lower zone, sloping away towards the property boundary, has a more natural feel and is seeded with a wildflower meadow which requires little water and maintenance, unlike the tidy gardens of more traditional suburban developments. *Carex texensis*, *Stipa tenuissima* (syn. *Nassella tenuissima*), *Nolina texana*, *Lupinus texensis*, *Eupatorium havanense*, *Viguiera stenoloba* and several agave and yucca species were used in the upper garden and along the stone pathway, with some scattered into the meadow area. Woody species at the perimeter include *Ulmus crassifolia*, *Quercus virginiana*, *Ilex decidua* and *Cercis canadensis* var. *texensis*, which are all drought- and heat-tolerant.

TEN EYCK LANDSCAPES

Designers: Ten Eyck Landscape Architects (TELA)

Location: El Paso, Texas and Austin, Texas, USA

Texas-based landscape architect Christy Ten Eyck specialises in sustainability in desert communities. For Christy, water has always been precious: her projects educate people to the path (or memory) of water. In an interview with The American Society of Landscape Architects (ASLA), Christy says, 'We need to come up with a new kind of beauty that expresses a tough, harsh landscape unique to its region.'

THE UNIVERSITY OF TEXAS AT EL PASO

This Campus transformation is emblematic of Ten Eyck Landscape Architects' (TELA) work to create spaces with a strong identity, while harvesting and filtrating rainwater.

El Paso is located on the banks of the Rio Grande, across the border from Mexico, in south-west Texas. The city lies within the Chihuahuan Desert at an altitude of 1,140 m (3,740 ft). The project changed the 4 ha (11 acre) site from a car-centric setting, characterised by parking lots covered in asphalt, to an inspiring, people-oriented, multifunctional landscape that offers a high quality of life and new heart of the campus. Academic buildings are visually connected to the desert using local rocks, reclaimed materials and native, drought-tolerant vegetation.

The 'Green Heart', Centennial Plaza, is an oval lawn area cut into what was an existing sloped parking lot,

bordered by seating steps on one side, forming an amphitheatre. New generous water harvesting arroyos were carved into the site surrounding the plaza and are planted with native Chihuahuan plants. The reclaimed Andesite boulder and earthen slopes along with planting surround the plaza and frame alleyways, paths and buildings. Two lawn areas within the new grounds minimise irrigation while providing outdoor recreation spaces. The native *Prosopis* spp. or mesquite tree, a medium-sized multi-stem species with yellow spring blossom, is used throughout, creating a human scale and welcome dappled shade.

Although average annual rainfall in El Paso is only 225 mm (8.8 in), many parts of the city are subject to occasional flooding during intense summer thunderstorms. Due to rain scarcity, stormwater flows are slowed down as much as possible through new planted arroyos and planted linear gardens or 'acequias' and allowed to absorb into the earth and recharge groundwater reserves. Topography and site levels were designed to convey water that used to run down sloped asphalt via these new arroyos and planted linear raingardens, celebrating rain-harvesting processes. Thanks to multiple sustainable choices implemented within the campus it now resonates with bird and insectlife.

The scheme received Silver certification in the Sustainable SITES Initiative rating system, and an honour award in the ASLA Professional Awards, 2023. *See pages 224-227.*

KINGSBURY COMMONS

Kingsbury Commons is the recreational heart in the southern 3 ha (7 acre) tip of Pease Park, a popular urban park stretching along Shoal Creek in downtown Austin, part of a renovation master plan.

Ten Eyck Landscape Architects (TELA) and team created new water and nature play areas, terraces around the repurposed Tudor Cottage, plazas, a new gateway, treehouse and multi-layered native plantings.

Clayton Korte Architects designed airy and rustic restrooms, storage buildings and steel mesh walls.

Great effort was made to divert a large portion of a natural spring's runoff from the adjacent street's storm gutter into a series of vegetated rain gardens and catchment basins, made of rock blocks that descend the slopes, making water harvesting processes a prominent feature within intimate seating areas.

Sustainable choices made in the master plan's design and renovation enabled this project to achieve Gold certification under the Sustainable SITES Initiative rating system. *See pages 228-229*

HOTEL MAGDALENA

On the same location as the former Terrace Motor Hotel, one of Austin's premier mid-century motor lodges, Hotel Magdalena has 89 rooms, spread across four towers in South Congress. Here, verdant, canyon-like interior courtyards between the hotel buildings feature a series of rain gardens traversed by pedestrian bridges. TELA set out to evoke the feeling of a laid-back lake house tucked into the dramatic geology of Austin. It's easy to forget this is a busy hotel complex.

Distinctive characteristics include several large existing *Quercus virginiana*, preserved and incorporated into the design, and a dramatic change in levels amplified by a planted retaining wall made of regional stone blocks. Every drop of water is appreciated; for example, diverse plantings of hardy native trees (*Taxodium distichum* and *Platanus mexicana*), shrubs and grasses are irrigated with stormwater runoff flowing into swales, and condensation water from the buildings' air-conditioning units is harvested.

As well as big vision projects, Austin needs relatively small projects to provide effective stormwater management, with the city located on the Colorado River, increasing the potential for flash floods.
See pages 230-231

PHOENIX GARDENS

Designers: Colwell Shelor Landscape Architects
Location: Phoenix, Arizona, USA

Arizona's capital is in the north-eastern reaches of the Sonoran Desert, the world's wettest desert, at the confluence of the Salt and Gila rivers; topography is primarily flat. Phoenix experiences some of the hottest temperatures of any city in the US, with very little rain and scorching summers. Principals Allison Colwell, Michele Shelor and their design studio are proponents of experimental design, with a deep appreciation for desert plant life and conservation in the low and high regions of Arizona.

HOUSE OF DESERT GARDENS

In the Paradise Valley neighbourhood, Colwell Shelor Landscape Architects converted this garden into a low water-use landscape. An array of desert plants from around the world is arranged in groups. The entrance garden is predominantly planted with candelabra and golden barrel (*Echinocactus grusonii*) cacti. A more spacious area features sizeable multi-stem ironwood trees (*Olneya tesota*) placed around a patio and underplanted with agaves.

This project celebrates diverse xeric vegetation while offering a new garden aesthetic for Phoenix that is resilient and sustainable, but also unapologetically man-made, particularly for those who still prefer formality, repetition and order. *See pages 232-237.*

GHOST WASH

The sloping 1 ha (2.5 acre) Paradise Valley property sits between two desert dry washes carrying stormwater from Camelback Mountain through the site to the valley below. (Desert dry wash is a North American vegetation type that lacks surface water for most of the year but is subject to periodic severe flooding events.)

Colwell Shelor Landscape Architects' redesign removed a water intensive 1970s plant palette, large lawn areas, and tall oleander hedges that closed off the property to its stunning views. An immersive garden of different 'galleries' with unique character, size and light exposure, uses plant species from arid regions around the world.

The front of the house features a more formal garden composed of cascading terraces and several washes, including a central core known as 'Ghost Wash' – an infrastructure amenity for stormwater collection

after which the property is named. An extensive floating roof captures stormwater which is conveyed to a tank, irrigating the lawn and adjacent vegetation. Perimeter washes flanking the property were restored and planted with native vegetation. A gradient of native and wild-looking vegetation decreases from the perimeter to the centre of the site.

The garden is surrounded by a permeable fence made of upright steel sticks or rebar allowing wildlife to come and go. An entrance garden features a grove of *Parkinsonia microphylla* among salvaged boulders and *Opuntia* spp. cacti. These species are also used along the public road on both sides of the fence, blending the garden into the surrounding Sonoran Desert flora.

The Ghost Wash project received an ASLA honour award for residential design in 2021, for advancing the aesthetic of gardens in Arizona and setting new sustainability standards. *See pages 238-243.*

LOS ANGELES GARDENS

Designers: Terremoto
Location: Los Angeles, California, USA

Terremoto (which means earthquake in Spanish and Italian) are forward-thinking and disruptive. Finding purpose in shaking up their discipline, co-founders David Godshall and Alain Peauroi believe the world is at a cultural, environmental and civilisational fork in the road. Projects challenge historical landscape architectural traditions and models, construction methods and materiality, while also celebrating the workers who construct their landscapes.

KX LAB

At KX LAB, Terremoto shift the city's aesthetic from an evergreen, irrigated, tropical-looking garden towards a space that reflects LA's desert climate. A loose, rocky, imprecise garden contrasts with the high precision, rigorous technology of knitting processes performed here.

Rich, diverse vegetation creates an oasis in the asphalt-dominated industrial neighbourhood. Over 20 native and drought-tolerant *Platanus racemosa* trees were planted. Native and adapted species were trialled, and observations used to amend the planting as necessary.

Repurposed concrete chunks are used as boulders, local gravel as the primary surface material, and reclaimed timber for seating. Aluminium tanks were installed to collect rainwater from the roof to irrigate the trees. The garden has no lawn but is fully covered by gravel and concrete pebbles that recall the look and atmosphere of a dry riverbed. Vegetation is planted within this mineral layer, which acts as mulch by suppressing weeds and retaining moisture in the soil.

Factory workers relax on benches positioned around a circular pond with native aquatic plants.
See pages 244-245.

LOS FELIZ TOWERS

This 14-storey twin tower was built in 1966 in the hillside LA neighbourhood of Los Feliz.

A first-floor pool deck spans and connects the whole area between two mid-century buildings, an important meeting place for the residential community. Terremoto was appointed by the board of residents to design drought-tolerant planting for large geometrical raised planters.

The result is a wild mix of regionally appropriate species of succulents and ground cover species juxtaposed against the orthogonal lines and symmetry of the flower beds. *Jacaranda mimosifolia*, *Parkinsonia florida* and *Acacia* spp. were used to replace the native *Lyonothamnus floribundus* var. *asplenifolius,* (commonly known as fernleaf Catalina ironwood), which were no longer performing well due to climate change.
See pages 246-247.

SAN FRANCISCO PENINSULA GARDENS

Designers: Surfacedesign, Inc.

Location: Woodside and Portola Valley, California, USA

Surfacedesign, Inc. is an award-winning, innovative landscape architecture and urban design firm based in San Francisco, led by partners James A. Lord, Roderick Wyllie and Geoff di Girolamo. The studio focuses on cultivating a sense of connection to the built and natural world, pushing people to engage with the landscape in new ways.

ULIVETO

The private Woodside residence nestles in sloping foothills of the Santa Cruz Mountains. A winding drive is lined with 150-year-old olive trees (saved from an unproductive orchard), gravel, dwarf olives, and rows of lavender. Xeric planting – an exotic collection of sculptural succulents and cacti – frames the entrance courtyard. A gently sculpted, naturalistic, perennial meadow features drought-tolerant Mediterranean and American natives, arranged in drifts. Floriferous perennials are intermingled among grasses and rush species such as bouteloua, eragrostis, schizachyrium or juncus, while *Carpinus betulus* trees provide formality. *See pages 248-251.*

GOLDEN OAK

Surfacedesign, Inc. drew inspiration for this eclectic composition of plants from a xeric Californian palette. Sculptural accent species throughout the garden were selected from regions with similar climates to Northern California's, for example, the owner's former home of New Zealand. Species are robust, requiring low water to thrive. The front lawn was replaced by a colourful mosaic of herbaceous plants and succulents. Exotic plants used along the formal entry walk decrease as you move to the property perimeter, where planting has a higher native species content and blends with endemic vegetation of evergreen oaks.

This novel plant community is unusual and exuberant, demonstrating an alternative waterwise approach to a Californian entrance garden. *See pages 252-253.*

CALIFORNIAN GARDENS

Designers: Ground Studio

Location: Carmel Valley and Woodside, California, USA

Ground Studio, founded by Bernard Trainor, is internationally recognised for elegantly crafted contextual Californian landscapes focused on ecological design and the encouragement of land regeneration. Through observation, listening and minimal intervention, they reveal the essence of place, inspiring a deep connection with land.

An avid gardener and successful painter, Bernard grew up in Australia on the Mornington Peninsula, where, surfing and sailing as a youngster he formed an early appreciation for design, landscape and light. After studying horticulture and garden design, he won a scholarship to England. Working with English plantswoman and garden designer Beth Chatto, he was inspired by her famous conversion of a grass parking area into a gravel garden.

Bernard relocated to Monterey, California and began his small landscape design firm in 2002, which later became Ground Studio. Together with partners David LeRoy, Ben Langford, Chris Merritt, and Johnson Bullard, the Ground Studio team has offices in Monterey, Napa and Santa Barbara.

GOODRICH TRAIL

Winner of a Merit Award for the Northern California chapter of the American Society of Landscape Architects Awards (ASLA), Goodrich Trail sits in a long, narrow valley in the foothills of the Santa Lucia range. Ground Studio's intentionally minimal design approach – first, understand the site's natural history – immerses its owners within the landscape. Redwood forest surrounding the property was disconnected from the house, so initial intervention added trees to allow multigenerational woodland to embrace the building.

Management of large grassland areas around the building aims to promote native perennial forbs and grasses while reducing exotic annual weeds not adapted to local conditions and prone to dry out quickly. Hardscape elements echoing the valley sit lightly within the native grassland. Rammed earth walls are used to define outdoor spaces and various sizes of concrete pavers are softened by poppies and yarrows growing in-between.

Overall, the approach is highly naturalistic, balanced against the needs of wildfire prevention, and shows a deep commitment to long-term stewardship of this wild oak savanna ecosystem. *See pages 254-259.*

ORCHARD HILL

On a former wagon stop along Santa Clara Valley, Orchard Hill sits on a clearing just below a native redwood forest. The primary goal was to maintain the site's rural character and blur the lines between garden and surroundings, maintaining sweeping views of the San Francisco Peninsula.

Ground Studio permeates domestic spaces with plants and seeks a new balance where humans are part of rather than dominating nature. Native grasslands were restored, running right up to the property edges,

with the swimming pool placed in the middle of a grassy orchard connecting to the house via a mowed path – what is natural and what is domestic are given equal weight.

Ground Studio's philosophy welcomes seasonality – including drought and vegetation dormancy – while upholding design that is restrained, natural, sustainable and in harmony with the environment.
See pages 260-263.

RANCHO 7

Rancho 7 in the Carmel Valley is an outstanding example of Ground Studio's approach to site-specific design. The 0.8 ha (2 acre) private home rests on an east-facing slope of the Santa Lucia Preserve.

Pacific fog greatly influences the mountain range's climate and endemic vegetation. Moisture is trapped on ocean-facing slopes, creating the right environment for rich woodlands of redwoods, *Sequoia sempervirens,* and oaks, *Quercus agrifolia*.

Land around the new house had been eroded,

exposed by construction works. Using nature as a guide, a first goal was to align the project within the environment by revegetating the landscape with redwoods of different sizes, bringing the forest closer to the contemporary private house of local stone and reclaimed redwood. Parts of its roof are green to collect and store stormwater. Topography conveys water along the hillside towards a catchment area between the house and parking lot, which is planted with moisture-loving multi-stem Betula nigra trees and Chondropetalum tectorum. Native grassland links the

garden with adjacent fields, with species such as Carex pansa, C. praegracilis, Nassella pulchra and N. cernua.

Minimal, careful interventions characterise the landscape design so that each man-made addition feels in tune with the site. The swimming pool is the most significant constructed feature, built within the meadow to immerse its users in nature. For Bernard, the tension between wild and designed spaces is where beauty and excitement reside. *See pages 264-265.*

THE POLLINATOR
AND BIRD GARDEN

Designers: Phyto Studio, in collaboration with Didier Design Studio and Lake Flato

Location: State College, Pennsylvania, USA

The Arboretum at Penn State was established for study and research by the Pennsylvania State University in State College, a municipality located in the centre of the state, surrounded by large tracts of farmland and forests.

The Arboretum was expanded several years ago by more than 60 per cent, adding the new 1.6 ha (4 acre) Pollinator and Bird Garden, designed by Thomas and Melissa Rainer, Emilie Carter and Claudia West (authors of *Planting in a Post-Wild World*), founders of Phyto Studio. The niche landscape architecture firm, in collaboration with Didier Design Studio and Lake Flato, created a garden with astounding diversity, designed in partnership with scientists from Penn State's Center for Pollinator Research, ornithology faculty, and other University and outside experts.

Maximising the variety and amount of wildlife the site could support was a first step, establishing different habitats such as forest, savanna, meadow, pond and orchard. In collaboration with university soil scientists, over seven different soil typologies were developed for each area, creating a high-diversity terrain.

Entomologists guided the slope grading to ensure it was appropriate for certain insect species to nest. Mulch materials were highly diversified throughout the garden to contribute to spatial complexity. Sand, gravel (in various gradings), expanded shale and shredded leaves were used to cover the soil.

Research results from Penn State and other universities helped identify high-performing herbaceous and woody plants that support insects, birds and other wildlife. *Zizia aurea*, *Pycnanthemum flexuosum*, *Solidago nemoralis*, *Claytonia virginica* and various asters, among others, score highly in supporting pollinators. The garden hosts an abundance of nearly 400 species and plant varieties; non-native plant species were also included to extend the flowering season and maximise pollen and nectar availability throughout the year.

NATIVE MEADOWS

Designers: Larry Weaner Landscape Associates (LWLA)

Location: Shermans Dale, Pennsylvania and Potomac, Maryland, USA

Philadelphia-based Larry Weaner Landscape Associates (LWLA) is recognised in the US for combining environmental science with the rich artistic traditions of landscape design. Founded by Larry Weaner in 1982, LWLA are known for their approach to creating and managing native landscapes, often in the form of meadows. Larry has received numerous awards for his work, including the 2021 Landscape Design Award from the American Horticulture Society.

THE BOWER

Home to William (an environmental engineer) and Jane Allis (an early childhood educator), The Bower (noun: a pleasant shady place; a retreat or sanctuary) is a native garden and sculpture park comprising a 2.4 ha (6 acre) meadow surrounded by 12 ha (30 acres) of woodland, in Perry County, Pennsylvania.

The site is a culmination of two lives well lived and shared together. The private and public sanctuary (open by appointment only), features woodlands, wetlands, lawns, meadows and gardens interspersed with sculptures and land art.

Oehme, van Sweden (OvS) designed the original site master plan in 2019, taking inspiration from the area's history, geology, hydrology and ecology, sitting within the Ridge and Valley ecoregion of the Appalachians, and the horizontal folding of Kittatinny Ridge.

In 2020 Larry Weaner Landscape Associates (LWLA) were appointed to develop planting communities across the site, focusing on creating garden spaces and meadows to support insects and birds, as well as humans.

For Larry, key to developing any planting strategy is understanding the amount of disturbance that has occurred historically on a site. Historical plant communities are more stable, with greater capacity to coexist over time. Novel plants, with less time to form relationships, tend to be more unstable and poorer from biodiversity, aesthetic and management standpoints. It was essential for Larry to avoid negatively impacting The Bower's existing high-quality, diverse vegetation.

The Bower, which opened in spring 2012 as an environment that enhances art while celebrating the historical plant community that characterises the site, was awarded first prize in the 2023 Land Ethics Award. *See pages 270-273.*

GLENSTONE

The Maryland art museum, north of Washington, DC, is a series of interconnected pavilions designed by architect Thomas Phifer, surrounded by 120 ha (300 acres) of landscape which features paths, trails, streams, meadows, forests and sculptures.

Larry Weaner Landscape Associates (LWLA) developed the painterly meadow planting in collaboration with Peter Walker and Partners from California (see Barangaroo on page 170) who conceived the overall landscape design. Heavily disturbed during construction, the land was seeded with different mixes using onsite historic plant communities. Larry explains that when seeding a meadow, two categories of plant species must be included in the mix: ruderal (first to colonise disturbed lands) and long-lived.

Different mixes were created for shady areas and sunny meadows. Herbaceous species native to Glenstone were intermingled with others from the Mid-Atlantic region.

The planted landscape now comprises 16 ha (40 acres) of seeded meadows and 18 ha (45 acres) of reforestation. More than 7,000 native trees were planted between 2013 and 2018.

Glenstone houses what many consider to be the greatest private collection of American and European contemporary art in the US. Owners Mitchell Rales and Emily Wei intend to encourage 'a state of mind created by the energy of architecture, the power of art, and the restorative qualities of nature'.

'Split-Rocker', a playful 37 ft tall flower sculpture by contemporary artist Jeff Koons, aligns three essential worlds of Glenstone: art, architecture and garden.
See pages 274-277

MARTIN LUTHER KING JR MEMORIAL LIBRARY ROOF GARDEN

Designers: Oehme, van Sweden (OvS)
Location: Washington, DC, USA

The Martin Luther King Jr Memorial Library, built in 1972 in downtown Washington, is a public building designed by notable modernist architect Mies van der Rohe. Of heavy construction, the library required modernisation without altering the original structure.

Oehme, van Sweden (OvS) landscape architects were appointed in 2015 to develop the project's landscape areas, joining the construction team of Mecanoo Architects, supported by local OTJ Architects.

Two extensive green roofs were created, the first, covering a newly constructed 2,675 sq m (28,800 sq ft) upper-level deck, is planted with drought-tolerant sedum to capture stormwater and help mitigate the heat-island effect, while serving as a viewing garden for dwellers of surrounding taller office buildings. The second roof, which also includes a drought-tolerant sedum carpet on the west side, transformed the fifth-floor flexible events and education space into a 1600 sq m (0.4 acre) public roof terrace.

Drought-tolerant grasses and perennials feature throughout. A native pollinator garden with regional species from the Mid-Atlantic provides color and wildlife value, while a sensory garden anchoring the southeast corner of the terrace provides texture and scent. A seasonal viewing garden at terrace entry features plants offering dramatic annual changes, and large swaths of ornamental grasses for winter structure. All planting areas sit within large, raised planters set back from the terrace perimeter, a requirement of the preservation rules of historic buildings that no plants be visible from street level.

This public roof garden in the middle of Washington DC, with its educational, immersive and aesthetic aspects, reaffirms the crucial role of such places for urban dwellers.

BROOKLYN GARDENS

Designers: Michael Van Valkenburgh Associates (MVVA)

Location: New York City, USA

Founded in 1982, Michael Van Valkenburgh Associates Inc (MVVA) has completed over 350 landscape design, construction, and restoration projects in both public and private realms. MVVA cultivates expertise in sustainability, soil toxicity, and waterfront infrastructure, and collaborates frequently with climate scientists, hydrologists, ecologists, artists, engineers and architects. The firm was chosen for two transformative city projects: Brooklyn Botanic Garden in 2010 and Brooklyn Bridge Park in 2008.

BROOKLYN BOTANIC GARDEN

The 21 ha (52 acre) garden in central Brooklyn, adjacent to Prospect Park, opened in 1911 as a public botanic garden for appreciation and scientific study.

MVVA has re-imagined the entire watershed, expanded it from 6 ha to 14 ha (15 acres to 36 acres). The ambitious Water Conservation Project has greatly reduced the garden's use of fresh water while also collecting stormwater runoff, reducing the pressure on Brooklyn's drainage system.

Water is filtered and recirculated from the existing upstream Japanese garden pond, through a new brook, (Belle's Brook) to a pond at the centre of the Shelby White and Leon Levy Water Garden, saving 83 million litres (21 million gallons) of fresh water annually. Ponds are lined with low-carbon bentonite clay, and bluestone boulders used along the brook and around the ponds were site-won materials. Bridges are constructed with locally grown *Robinia* timber. *See pages 284-285.*

BROOKLYN BRIDGE PARK

Formerly a long stretch of derelict piers lining the waterfront, Brooklyn Bridge Park is a shining example of place making in a dense urban environment. Extending 2 km (1.3 miles) along the lower Manhattan waterfront, the 35 ha (85 acre) park offers spectacular views of the Brooklyn and Manhattan bridges, East River, lower Manhattan skyline and New York Harbour.

Since 2008, the site has been gradually transformed and repurposed by the Brooklyn Bridge Park Corporation, the initial concept derived from strong public opposition to building apartment towers at the water's edge.

Setting a benchmark for waterfront projects worldwide, Michael Van Valkenburgh Associates reconnected the city to its harbour through thoughtful design and ingenious landscape solutions, with the added provision of storm buffers in an age of climate change and rising sea levels.

In October 2012, the park's storm resilience was tested by the devastating effects of Hurricane Sandy, which twice flooded low-lying areas with 0.9 m (3 ft) of seawater. Tree losses due to flooding included *Platanus* x *acerifolia* 'Bloodgood' and *Metasequoia glyptostroboides*. This unexpected event allowed landscape architects to assess which species were storm resilient, guiding planting palettes for future phases.

Today, the park attracts more than 5 million people annually, and features a vast array of spaces and amenities. On top of renovated piers, a perennial meadow attracts insects and wildlife in the middle of summer (Pier 6); ponds collect and filter stormwater and create a freshwater wetland habitat (Pier 1); old warehouses were partially deconstructed to make space for multiple playing fields (Pier 2).

Diverse habitat-specific and wild-looking plantings are visible throughout the park. Fully vegetated sound-deflecting steep berms were constructed along the park's eastern edge to shelter the site from the noise of the adjacent Brooklyn-Queens Expressway.

A standout for this project is the number of structures, elements and materials repurposed and recycled, showing a high level of sustainability, connecting the new park with its past harbour history.

Reclaimed granite slabs and blocks, salvaged from the Roosevelt Island Bridge and Willis Avenue Bridge reconstruction, were used for paving and seating walls, and longleaf pine timber beams from a cold storage warehouse were used for benches. Mooring cleats were salvaged and repurposed as play elements, and a wooden pile field left in place, helped to buffer a constructed salt marsh from wave action.
See pages 286-289.

DOMINO PARK

Designers: James Corner Field Operations
Location: Brooklyn, New York City

Domino Park is a 2 ha (5 acre) waterfront public park in the Williamsburg neighbourhood of Brooklyn, spanning 400 m (1300 ft) along the East River on the former Domino Sugar Refinery site, with iconic views of Brooklyn Bridge.

Designed by James Corner Field Operations (designers of the Manhattan High Line), the park aims to reconnect the urban fabric of Williamsburg to the water while celebrating its industrial history through recycling structures and materials. Relics reclaimed from the sugar refinery (such as metal columns, cranes, screw conveyors and syrup tanks) were repurposed into play elements or walkaways, while seating is made from recycled timber from the refinery.

With stunning views of the Manhattan skyline, an extensive events program, and diverse play, sport and recreational facilities, the park was embraced by the Williamsburg community, and has had over 3.5 million visitors since opening in 2018.

ROBIN HILL

Designer: Dan Pearson Studio
Location: Norfolk, Connecticut, USA

Robin Hill, a 1920s neo-Georgian brick mansion with 8 ha (20 acres) of landscape and garden, had fallen into neglect, with large portions returned to woodland. Current owners Susan Sheehan and John O'Callaghan were unsure about what to do with its wild spaces and turned to British landscape designer Dan Pearson after reading his book *Spirit: Garden Inspiration*.

Not so much a garden, Susan wanted an environment. The seamless boundaries between cultivated and uncultivated are a defining characteristic of Robin Hill.

Dan is mindful of the delicate balance between nature and horticulture, and says observing the vegetation, light and seasonal rhythms is key to recognising a unique sense of place.

His vision re-exposed the original bones of the garden, extending it into the landscape with meadows, clearings and planting interventions. Terraces were added around the house in local stone, together with a cutting garden, moss garden and three meadows. A new system of trails through the forest connects the house

with the wider site while enabling Susan and John to discover areas previously overgrown and impenetrable. A number of sculptural insertions in the landscape, including a dry stone cone and a tapered wall, direct the eye towards focal points within the woodland and encourage you to explore further.

Most plants introduced are native, carefully selected to enhance local biodiversity. Some non-native species were added for greater plant diversity and to complement the atmosphere: a glade of *Stewartia pseudocamellia* at the edge of the woods, and a group of *Cercidiphyllum japonicum* in the moss garden.

Five years ago, James McGrath, head gardener at Robin Hill, was convinced by Dan's approach to take on his 'dream job' after working in gardens around the world – in England, Spain, the Netherlands and Jerusalem. All materials produced on site are used in a closed loop; plants are mowed down, and shredded foliage is used as mulch. Irrigation is used only to establish new plants. Because the property is not fenced, the wild is welcomed, with visits from bears, deer and porcupines, among others.

Dan's vision, Susan and John's commitment, and James's love for Robin Hill have created a landscape that whispers rather than shouts.

SUMMERHOME GARDEN

Designers: Lisa Negri and Kevin Philip Williams
Location: Denver, Colorado, USA

Lisa Negri, the former CEO of an environmental engineering company, met Kevin Williams, a horticulturist and garden designer, while volunteering at Denver Botanic Gardens (see page 298), a five-minute drive from home. Concerned about the increasing replacement of the mid-century aesthetic of a bungalow neighbourhood and their gardens by oversized contemporary farmhouses, in 2019 Lisa bought the house next door to save it from inappropriate development.

Initially she was unsure how to use the property, but soon realised she wanted open space, and had the house demolished to make room for a public park designed by Kevin.

Deeply interested in naturalistic gardens, Kevin thought the plot – a standard city lot of 38 m by 15 m (125 ft by 50 ft) – offered an opportunity to reflect the southwestern US landscapes loved by Lisa. SummerHome Garden was modelled on the Colorado shrub steppe, using waterwise species readily available in local nurseries. This is not a native garden, rather one that showcases regionally adapted species forming a novel plant community suited to Denver's semi-arid, high-altitude climate.

Once the house was demolished, foundations were left in place and covered with soil. Over 4,000 plants were laid out by Kevin, planted by volunteers. Many herbaceous species were sourced as bare-root plants, with almost 100 per cent survival rate. Among the garden's initial 45 species (Lisa now estimates there to be approximately 92) are *Achnatherum calamagrostis* 'Undaunted', *Andropogon hallii*, *Diascia integerrima*, *Phacelia campanularia*, *Baptisia alba* and various salvia species. Once established, plants are left to thrive with natural rainfall.

In the hottest, sunniest corner of the garden, a crevice bed with xeric plants was constructed with 27 tonnes (30 tons) of Colorado sandstone – scrap material from a local quarry. Paths were covered with gravel, and planting areas mulched with expanded shale, both sourced locally.

Now open to the public, the garden has become a joyful gathering place, attracting locals who visit regularly and participate in maintaining the garden.

DENVER BOTANIC GARDENS

Designer: Panayoti Kelaidis
Location: Denver, Colorado, USA

Located at high elevation, roughly in the middle of the US, Denver has a peculiar climate; a mixture of steppe, desert and maritime influences all merging – a unique opportunity for horticultural diversity. However, a more traditional, water-intensive aesthetic model has influenced the region's public and private landscapes for decades.

Panayoti Kelaidis is senior curator and director of Outreach at Denver Botanic Gardens, where he has demonstrated a sustainable approach to horticulture for many years. A third of Denver Botanic Gardens is maintained with low or no water. While native, steppe, hardy succulents and cactus gardens help visitors develop a taste for dry and naturalistic gardens, Panayoti admits that more work needs to be done to shift preferences from lush, green and 'tidy' yards to xeriscapes.

Through helping to establish Plant Select (a non-profit collaboration between Colorado State University, Denver Botanic Gardens and professional horticulturists), Panayoti is actively contributing to this shift.

Smart plant choices inspired by the Rocky Mountains region are encouraged: tough, resilient, non-invasive, insect- and disease-resistant plants, with the ability to thrive with little water after the establishment period.

One of the top five botanic gardens in the US, Denver Botanic Gardens – and other horticultural institutions, such as the Gardens on Spring Creek – are crucial to changing public perception of how gardens should look in Colorado.

Panayoti believes in the power of new public projects (such as the High Line in New York and Lurie Garden in Chicago) to change people's tastes and influence others to follow. With climate change, he says a shift to a new kind of planting is inevitable.

THE GARDENS ON SPRING CREEK

Designers: Lauren Springer and Bryan Fischer
Location: Fort Collins, Colorado, USA

'The Gardens on Spring Creek' is a 7.3 ha (18 acre) community botanical garden, owned and managed by the city of Fort Collins in Colorado. Bryan Fischer, curator of the plant collection, is also responsible for a prairie garden and rock plant display.

In 2018, volunteers helped plant a native meadow with prairie plants on a 2,000 sq m (0.5 acre) area of the gardens. While Bryan's vision for this project came directly from meadows of the Rocky Mountains, he distilled their essence into an urban garden setting with an idealised representation of wild vegetation. Planting features a matrix of intermingled, naturalistic prairie plants mixed with under-used, lesser-known native species with the potential for garden cultivation (not yet extensively tested in the region). Three main designed prairie plant community mixes respond to terrain alterations: short grass in the dry areas on top of low mounds; tall grass in dish-shaped depressions; and mesic grass on the gentle slopes.

Ninety per cent of plants are native species requiring minimal watering, and no fertilising. Planting areas are mowed in early spring, with shredded biomass left on the ground to improve heavy soil texture.

Garden designer Lauren Springer was engaged to design and plant a 3,000 sq m (0.75 acre) zone of 'The Gardens on Spring Creek', called 'The Undaunted Garden' after her bestselling book *The Undaunted Garden: Planting for Weather-Resilient Beauty*. It's been a long-held professional dream of this pioneering plantswoman to work in a public space and freely create, steward and share a complex planting.

Resilient plants also offer wildlife and pollinator benefits. Planted in 2019 and 2020, areas are irrigated when needed during dry spells in the hottest summer months, and newly planted plants are hand watered to avoid over watering the mature established denizens.

The garden is divided into four areas that flow seamlessly into each other. The first: a south-facing slope dedicated to unusual cold-hardy cacti – the largest collection in the US with more than 300 cacti of various species. The second: a western cottage garden, reinterpreting the floriferous English cottage gardens with western-adapted, drought-tolerant plants. The third: an artificial rocky site using rubble left behind after construction, mixed with soil from the existing site and planted with small, low-growing Mediterranean and Rocky Mountain native species.

The last part of Lauren's garden is inspired by the chaparral, a shrubland plant community found in areas with Mediterranean climates in Arizona, Texas, California and Oregon. This area features mostly western North American shrubs and subshrubs intermingled with yuccas, grasses and perennials combined to create a wild and romantic composition where visitors can find ideas for their own gardens. Some representative species used are *Yucca baccata*, *Artemisia filifolia*, *Arctostaphylos* x *coloradoensis*, *A. patula*, *Gutierrezia sarothrae* and *Ericameria nauseosa*.

In 'The Undaunted Garden', Lauren combines different styles and plants (western native species and well-adapted non-natives) to create an educational urban garden appropriate for the Fort Collins climate. *See pages 306-309.*

LAUREN SPRINGER'S
HOME GARDEN

For her own garden, Lauren Springer wanted a wild garden that distilled the essence of the nearby Rocky Mountains landscape. Her naturalistic and textural style is informed by what she sees as 'necessity': to reflect the challenges of location and an ever more extreme climate.

'I think there's a lot to learn from hard-scrabble planting in a ferocious climate with lean soil,' says Lauren. 'We've had to be pioneers with our plant choices for a long time.'

The biggest challenge came in blending the garden harmoniously with the surrounding mountainous terrain. 'Textures, forms and subtle non-flower colours have their own beauty and offer a big lesson in gardening in extremes,' says Lauren. While the lush, floral feel of more generous and temperate northern hemisphere climates occurs in May/June, she prefers the beauty in her garden in late summer and autumn, with its wide view where light comes to play.

With the help of friends, to help place about 25 tons of rock, Lauren started her 1.5 ha (4 acre) home garden four years ago. One quarter of it is dedicated to the wild short-grass prairie, and another to mixed plantings with trees, shrubs, hardy cacti, small bulbs, native wildflowers, and herbaceous plants (mainly native species) to increase diversity and wildlife – Lauren feels a duty to create an oasis for all creatures in tune with the environment.

Many of the plants were propagated by Lauren through cuttings and seeds collected in the wild. She has also introduced several plants in the trade, such as *Muhlenbergia reverchonii* 'Undaunted', *M. rigens* 'Girl Next Door', *Oenothera fremontii* 'Shimmer', *Salvia greggii* hybrid 'Ultra Violet' and *Epilobium canum* 'Flame Thrower'.

Although the garden is planted with species that don't need additional irrigation after establishment, Lauren carefully manages their watering needs during drought.

Although the garden is still only half finished, Lauren isn't stressed; she enjoys the ongoing nature of editing, nurturing and being in the garden. Although young, it has already achieved a unique North American plain and mountain voice. Just like Lauren's: quiet, subtle, yet strong. *See pages 310-317.*

LIST OF GARDENS

AFRICA

Azaren, p.114
Designer: Eric Ossart and Arnaud Maurières (O+M)
Location: Tnine Ourika, Morocco
Average summer high +37.2 °C (99.0 °F);
winter low +5.8 °C (42.4 °F)
31° 37' 48" N
466 m (1529 ft) elevation
220 mm (8.67 in) average yearly rainfall

AUSTRALIA & NEW ZEALAND

Among Tall Trees, p.194
Designers: Mark and Kerryn Fountain
Location: Mount Rumney, Tasmania, Australia
Average summer high +22.7 °C (72.86 °F);
winter low +5.2 °C (41.36 °F)
42° 52' 50" S
17 m (56 ft) elevation
563 mm (22.16 in) average yearly rainfall

Australian Gardens, p.138
Designer: Phillip Johnson Landscapes
Location: Euroa and Olinda, Victoria, Australia
Average summer high +29.6 °C (85.28 °F);
winter low +4.1 °C (39.2 °F)
36° 45' 0" S
175 m (574 ft) elevation
651 mm (25.6 in) average yearly rainfall

Barangaroo, p.174
Designer: Peter Walker and David Walker,
PWP Landscape Architecture /
Johnson Pilton Walker (JPW)
Location: Sydney, New South Wales, Australia
Average summer high +27 °C (80.6 °F);
winter low +8.9 °C (48 °F)
33° 52' 4" S
0–39 m (0–128 ft) elevation
1149 mm (45.26 in) average yearly rainfall

Garden for the Future, p.162
Designer: T.C.L (Taylor Cullity Lethlean)/Paul Thompson
Location: Bendigo, Victoria, Australia
Average summer high +30.2 °C (86.4 °F);
winter low +2.7 °C (36.9 °F)
36° 45' 0" S
213 m (699 ft) elevation
512 mm (20.17 in) average yearly rainfall

Glenluce Garden, p.166
Designer: Michael Wright and Catherine Rush
(Rush Wright Associates)
Location: Glenluce, Victoria, Australia
Average summer high +28.3 °C (82.9 °F);
winter low +3.4 °C (38.1 °F)
37° 3' 49" S
310 m (1020 ft) elevation
586 mm (23.11 in) average yearly rainfall

Melbourne City Garden, p.158
Designer: Amanda Oliver Gardens
Location: Melbourne, Victoria, Australia
Average summer high +26.6 °C (79.88 °F);
winter low +5.4 °C (41.72 °F)
37° 48' 51" S
113 m (37 ft) elevation
541 mm (21.29 in) average yearly rainfall

Mornington Garden, p.146
Designer: Jane Jones Landscapes
Location: Mornington, Victoria, Australia
Average summer high +25 °C (77 °F);
winter low +6.5 °C (43.7 °F)
38° 13' 40" S
60 m (196 ft) elevation
740 mm (29.13 in) average yearly rainfall

Mt Pisa Garden, p.200
Designer: Jo Wakelin
Location: Mt Pisa, Central Otago, New Zealand
Average summer high +24.4 °C (75.9 °F);
winter low –1.5 °C (29.3 °F)
45° 2' 24" S
296 m (971 ft) elevation
390 mm (15.4 in) average yearly rainfall

Spring Bay Mill, p.182
Designer: Marcus Ragus (Verdant Way)
Location: Triabunna, Tasmania, Australia
Average summer high +22.2 °C (71.96 °F);
winter low +3.6 °C (38.48 °F)
42° 30' 0" S
14 m (45.9 ft) elevation
674 mm (26.53 in) average yearly rainfall

Sydney Metro Planting Trial, p.180
Designer: Jon Hazelwood, (Hassell)
Location: Sydney, New South Wales, Australia
Average summer high +27 °C (80.6 °F);
winter low +8.9 °C (48 °F)
33° 52' 4" S
39 m (128 ft) elevation
1149 mm (45.26 in) average yearly rainfall

Tasmanian Coastal Landscape, p.188
Designer: Jennie and Rob Churchill
Location: Dolphin Sands, Tasmania, Australia
Average summer high +22.2 °C (71.96 °F);
winter low +3.6 °C (38.48 °F)
42 4' 57" S
6 m (20 ft) elevation
593 mm (23.34 in) average yearly rainfall

The Family Garden, p.152
Designer: Jo Ferguson
Location: Flinders, Victoria, Australia
Average summer high +25 °C (77 °F);
winter low +6.5 °C (43.7 °F)
38° 13' 40" S
60 m (196 ft) elevation
740 mm (29.13 in) average yearly rainfall

Trentham Garden, p.160
Designer: Simon Rickard
Location: Trentham, Victoria, Australia
Average summer high +23.2 °C (73.76 °F);
winter low +2.5 °C (36.5 °F)
37° 23' 0" S
700 m (2297 ft) elevation
1110 mm (43.74 in) average yearly rainfall

Wildcoast, p.150
Designer: Sam Cox
Location: Portsea, Victoria, Australia
Average summer high +22.8 °C (73.04 °F);
winter low +6.5 °C (43.7 °F)
38° 19' 12" S
10 m (32 ft) elevation
740 mm (29.13 in) average yearly rainfall

Yalamurra, p.170
Designer: Kurt Wilkinson
Location: Adelaide Hills, South Australia, Australia
Average summer high +30 °C (86 °F);
winter low +7.7 °C (45.86 °F)
34° 55' 39" S
300 m (980 ft) elevation
536 mm (21.10 in) average yearly rainfall

EUROPE

Almere, p.82
Designer: Lianne Pot
Location: Almere, Netherlands
Average summer high +21.8 °C (71.2 °F);
winter low +1.5 °C (34.7 °F)
52° 22' 0" N
−3 m (−10 ft) elevation
846 mm (33.3 in) average yearly rainfall

Amsterdam Public Plantings, p.70
Designers: Ton Muller and the city municipality of Amsterdam
Location: Amsterdam, Netherlands
Average summer high +22.5 °C (72.5 °F);
winter low +1.2 °C (34.2 °F)
52° 22' 0" N
0 m (0 ft) elevation
850 mm (33.46 in) average yearly rainfall

Avila Garden, p.6
Designer: Renate Kastner and Miguel Urquijo
(Urquijo-Kastner Studio)
Location: Ávila, Spain
Average summer high +28.5 °C (83.3 °F);
winter low −1.6 °C (29.1 °F)
40° 39' 0" N
1132 m (3714 ft) elevation
416 mm (16.04 in) average yearly rainfall

Copenhagen Landscapes, p.90
Designer: SLA
Location: Copenhagen, Denmark
Average summer high +22.2 °C (72.0 °F);
winter low −0.8 °C (30.6 °F)
55° 40' 34" N
1–91 m (1–298 ft) elevation
685 mm (26.9 in) average yearly rainfall

Dehesa el Milagro, p.22
Designer: Clara Muñoz-Rojas and Belén Moreu (Muñoz y Moreu)
Location: Alcañizo, Toledo, Spain
Average summer high +34.6 °C (94.3 °F);
winter low +1.3 °C (34.3 °F)
39° 57' 30'' N
373 m (1223 ft)
342 mm (13 in) average yearly rainfall

German Gardens, p.104
Designer: Harald Sauer
Location: Ludwigshafen and Mannheim, Germany
Average summer high +27.5 °C (81.5 °F);
winter low +1.0 °C (33.8 °F)
49° 28' 52" N
96 m (315 ft) elevation
629 mm (24.78 in) average yearly rainfall

Grasse garden, p.40
Designers: James Basson (Scape Design)
Location: Grasse, Provence-Alpes-Côte d'Azur, France
Average summer high +24.8 °C (76.6 °F);
winter low −0.6 °C (30.9 °F)
43° 40' 0" N
80–1061 m (262–3481 ft) elevation
982 mm (38.6 in) average yearly rainfall

Greek Gardens, p.60
Designer: Thomas Doxiadis (doxiadis+)
Location: Athens and Antiparos, Greece
Average summer high +34.3 °C (93.7 °F);
winter low +7.1 °C (44.8 °F)
37° 59' 3" N
70–308 m (30–1010 ft) elevation
433 mm (17.06 in) average yearly rainfall

Ibiza Gardens, p.24
Designer: Juan Masedo
Location: Ibiza, Spain
Average summer high +29.7 °C (85.46 °F);
winter low +8.1 °C (46.58 °F)
38° 58' 48" N
0–475 m (1558 ft) elevation
413 mm (16.25 in) average yearly rainfall

Jaktgatan and Lövängsgatan, Norra Djurgårdsstaden, p.102
Designer: AJ Landskap
Location: Stockholm, Sweden
Average summer high +23.6 °C (74.5 °F);
winter low −2.9 °C (26.8 °F)
59° 19' 46" N
28 m (92 ft) elevation
546 mm (21.51 in) average yearly rainfall

Klinta Garden, p.94
Designer: Peter Korn
Location: Höör, Sweden
Average summer high +23.2 °C (73.8 °F);
winter low −1.2 °C (29.8 °F)
55° 42' 14" N
86m (282 ft) elevation
676 mm (26.62 in) average yearly rainfall

La Granja Alnardo, p.18
Designer: Tom Stuart-Smith
Location: Ribera del Duero, Spain
Average summer high +28 °C (82 °F);
winter low −1 °C (30.2 °F)
41° 41' 0" N
800 m (2624 ft) elevation
450 mm (17.71 in) average yearly rainfall

Le Jardin Champêtre, p.32
Designer: Imogen Checketts and Kate Dumbleton
Location: Caunes-Minervois, France
Average summer high +28.6 °C (83.5 °F);
winter low +3.1 °C (37.6 °F)
43° 19' 39" N
190 m (623 ft) elevation
648 mm (25.53 in) average yearly rainfall

Le Jardin Sec, p.36
Designers: Olivier and Clara Filippi
Location: Loupian, Montpellier, France
Average summer high +29.5°C (85.1 °F);
winter low 3.3 °C (37.9°F)
43° 36' 42.84" N
7–121 m (23–397 ft) elevation
639 mm (25.17 in) average yearly rainfall

Max IV Laboratory Landscape, p.100
Designer: Snohetta
Location: Lund, Sweden
Average summer high +23.2 °C (73.8 °F);
winter low −1.2 °C (29.8 °F)
55° 42' 14" N
86 m (282 ft) elevation
676 mm (26.62 in) average yearly rainfall

Netherlands Gardens, p.74
Designer: Arjan Boekel
Location: Heiloo and Landsmeer, Netherlands
Average summer high +22.5 °C (72.5 °F);
winter low +1.2 °C (34.2 °F)
52° 36' 0" N
3 m (10 ft) elevation
850 mm (33.46 in) average yearly rainfall

Nieuw-Haamstede Garden, p.86
Designer: Piet Oudolf, in collaboration with
Tom de Witte
Location: Nieuw-Haamstede, Netherlands
Average summer high +22.5°C (72.5 °F);
winter low +1.2 °C (34.2 °F)
52° 21' 0" N
1 m (3 ft) elevation
850 mm (33.48 in) average yearly rainfall

Ruin Garden, p.110
Designer: Anselm Reyle, Tanja Lincke and
Das Reservat
Location: Berlin, Germany
Average summer high +25 °C (77 °F);
winter low −1.9 °C (28.6 °F)
52° 31' 12" N
48 m (157 ft) elevation
570 mm (22 in) average yearly rainfall

South of France Gardens, p.40
Designer: James Basson (Scape Design)
Location: Maussane-les-Alpilles, Grasse and
Tourerettes-sur-Loup, southern France
Average summer high +29.5 °C (85.1 °F);
winter low +2.5 °C (36.5 °F)
43° 43' 18" N
0–342 m (0–1122 ft) elevation
580 mm (22.84 in) average yearly rainfall

**Stavros Niarchos Foundation Cultural
Center and Park, p.48**
Designer: Deborah Nevins & Associates and
H. Pangalou & Associates
Location: Athens, Greece
Average summer high +34.3 °C (93.7 °F);
winter low +7.1 °C (44.8 °F)
37° 59' 3" N
70–308 m (30–1010 ft) elevation
433 mm (17.06 in) average yearly rainfall

Tatoi Club & The Rooster, p.54
Designer: H. Pangalou & Associates
Location: Athens and Antiparos, Greece
Average summer high +34.3 °C (93.7 °F);
winter low +7.1 °C (44.8 °F)
37° 59' 3" N
70–308 m (30–1010 ft) elevation
433 mm (17.06 in) average yearly rainfall

Toledo Garden, p.14
Designer: Fernando Martos
Location: Talavera de la Reina, Spain
Average summer high +34.6 °C (94.3 °F);
winter low +1.3 °C (34.3 °F)
39° 57' 30" N
373 m (1223 ft) elevation
342 mm (13.46 in) average yearly rainfall

Tourrettes-sur-loup garden, p.40
Designer: James Basson (Scape Design)
Location: Tourrettes-sur-Loup, Alpes-
Maritimes, France
Average summer high +26.1 °C (79 °F);
winter low +2.6 °C (36.6 °F)
43° 43' 0" N
47–1246 m (154–4088 ft) elevation
982 mm (38.6 in) average yearly rainfall

UNITED KINGDOM

Kingswear Garden, P.126
Designer: Duncan Nuttall and AMELD
Location: Kingswear, Devon, England
Average summer high +18.4 °C (65.2 °F);
winter low +5.7 °C (42.3 °F)
50° 20' 52" N
84 m (276 ft) elevation
870 mm (34.25 in) average yearly rainfall

**Kitchen Garden at RHS Garden
Bridgewater, p.136**
Designer: Charlotte Harris and Hugo Bugg of
Harris Bugg Studio
Location: Salford, Manchester, England
Average summer high +20.01°C (68 °F);
winter low +1.5 °C (34.7 °F)
53° 28' 58" N
54 m (177 ft) elevation
1197 mm (47.13 in) average yearly rainfall

Knepp Castle Estate, p.118
Designer: Tom Stuart-Smith, James
Hitchmough, Mick Crawley
Location: West Grinstead, West Sussex,
England
Average summer high +23.14 °C (73.6 °F);
winter low +1.5 °C (34.7 °F)
50° 58' 26" N
127 m (417 ft) elevation
833 mm (32.8 in) average yearly rainfall

Meadow Garden, p.132
Designer: Jo McKerr
Location: Wellow, Somerset, England
Average summer high +21.8 °C (71.2 °F);
winter low +2.2 °C (35.9 °F)
51° 22' 48" N
25–238 m (82–780 ft) elevation
829 mm (32.63 in) average yearly rainfall

Wakehurst, p.130
Designer: Larry Weaner Landscape
Associates (LWLA)
Location: Haywards Heath, West Sussex,
England
Average summer high +20.8 °C (69.4 °F);
winter low +2.5 °C (36.4 °F)
51° 0' 17" N
49 m (160 ft) elevation
763 mm (30 in) average yearly rainfall

Wudston House, p.124
Designer: James Hitchmough
Location: Wedhampton, Wiltshire, UK
Average summer high +21.8°C (71.2 °F); winter
low +1.6 °C (34.8°F)
51° 20' 0" N
132 m (433 ft) elevation
798 mm/year (31.41 in) average yearly rainfall

UNITED STATES OF AMERICA

Brooklyn Gardens, p.284
Designer: Michael Van Valkenburgh
Associates (MVVA)
Location: New York City, USA
Average summer high +29.4 °C (84.9 °F);
winter low −2.3 °C (27.9 °F)
40° 42' 46" N
10 m (33 ft) elevation
1258 mm (49.52 in) average yearly rainfall

Californian Gardens, p.254
Designer: Ground Studio
Location: Carmel Valley and Woodside,
California, USA
Average summer high +25.8 °C (78.5 °F);
winter low +4.4 °C (40 °F)
36° 28' 38" N
258 m (846 ft) elevation
456 mm (17.94 in) average yearly rainfall

Coleson Bruce Garden, p.218
Designer: Coleson Bruce and John Ignacio
Location: Austin, Texas, USA
Average summer high +35.1 °C (95.2 °F);
winter low +5.8 °C (42.6 °F)
30° 26' 72" N
289–1450 ft (88–405 m) elevation
921 mm (36.25 in) average yearly rainfall

Denver Botanic Gardens, p.302
Designer: Panayoti Kelaidis
Location: Denver, Colorado, USA
Average summer high +32.2 °C (89.9 °F);
winter low −7.4 °C (18.7 °F)
39° 44' 21" N
1564–1734 m (5130–5690 ft) elevation
368 mm (14.48 in) average yearly rainfall

Domino Park, p.290
Designer: James Corner Field Operations
Location: Brooklyn, New York City, USA
Average summer high +29.4 °C (84.9 °F);
winter low −2.3 °C (27.9 °F)
40° 42' 46" N
10 m (33 ft) elevation
1258 mm (49.52 in) average yearly rainfall

Glenstone, p.274
Designer: Larry Weaner Landscape
Associates (LWLA)
Location: Potomac, Maryland, USA
Average summer high +29.4 °C (85 °F);
winter low −2.8 °C (27 °F)
39° 1' 0" N
110 m (361 ft) elevation
1024 mm (40.26 in) average yearly rainfall

**Lauren Springer's Home Garden,
p.310**
Designer: Lauren Springer
Location: Fort Collins, Colorado, USA
Average summer high +30.8 °C (87.4 °F);
winter low −7.6 °C (18.3 °F)
40° 33' 33" N
1525 m (5003 ft) elevation
402 mm (15.88 in) average yearly rainfall

Los Angeles Gardens, p.244
Designer: Terremoto
Location: Los Angeles, California, USA
Average summer high +27.6 °C (81.7 °F);
winter low +10.5 °C (50.9 °F)
34° 03' 08" N
305 ft (93 m) elevation
206 mm (8.12 in) average yearly rainfall

**Martin Luther King Jr Memorial
Library Roof Garden, p.278**
Designer: Oehme, van Sweden (OvS)
Location: Washington, DC, USA
Average summer high +32.0 °C (89.6 °F);
winter low −1.1 °C (30.1 °F)
38° 54' 17" N
0–125 m (0–409 ft) elevation
1062 mm (41.82 in) average yearly rainfall

Native Meadows, p.270
Designer: Larry Weaner Landscape
Associates (LWLA)
Location: Shermans Dale, Pennsylvania, USA
Average summer high +30.4 °C (86.8 °F);
winter low −5.0 °C (23 °F)
40° 19' 27" N
143 m (468 ft) elevation
1123 mm (44.23 in) average yearly rainfall

Peralta Lane Garden, p.222
Designer: Amy Hovis (Eden Garden Design)
Location: Austin, Texas, USA
Average summer high +35.1 °C (95.2 °F);
winter low +5.8 °C (42.6 °F)
30° 26' 72" N
88–405 m (289–1450 ft) elevation
921 mm (36.25 in) average yearly rainfall

Phoenix Gardens, p.232
Designer: Colwell Shelor Landscape
Architects
Location: Phoenix, Arizona, USA
Average summer high +39.7 °C (103.6 °F);
winter low +8.6 °C (47.5 °F)
33° 26' 54" N
1086 ft (331 m) elevation
128 mm (5.04 in) average yearly rainfall

Robin Hill, p.292
Designer: Dan Pearson Studio
Location: Norfolk, Connecticut, USA
Average summer high +27.2 °C (81 °F);
winter low −7.7 °C (18 °F)
41° 59' 1" N
375 m (1230 ft) elevation
820 mm (32.31 in) average yearly rainfall

**San Francisco Peninsula Gardens,
p.248**
Designer: Surfacedesign, Inc.
Location: Woodside and Portola Valley,
California, USA
Average summer high +22.6 °C (72.7 °F);
winter low +8 °C (46.4 °F)
37° 22' 30"
140 m (459 ft) elevation
785 mm (30.9 in) average yearly rainfall

SummerHome Garden, p.298
Designer: Lisa Negri and Kevin Philip Williams
Location: Denver, Colorado, USA
Average summer high +32.2 °C (89.9 °F);
winter low −7.4 °C (18.7 °F)
39° 44' 21" N
1564–1734 m (5130–5690 ft) elevation
368 mm (14.48 in) average yearly rainfall

Ten Eyck Landscapes, p.224
Designers: Ten Eyck Landscape Architects
(TELA)
Location: El Paso, Texas and Austin Texas,
USA
Average summer high +35.1 °C (95.2 °F);
winter low +5.8 °C (42.6 °F)
30° 26' 72" N
289–1450 ft (88–405 m) elevation
921 mm (36.25 in) average yearly rainfall

The Gardens on Spring Creek, p.306
Designer: Lauren Springer and Bryan Fischer
Location: Fort Collins, Colorado, USA
Average summer high 30.8 °C (87.4 °F);
winter low −7.6 °C (18.3 °F)
40° 33' 33" N
1525 m (5003 ft) elevation
402 mm (15.88 in) average yearly rainfall

The Pollinator and Bird Garden, p.266
Designer: Phyto Studio, in collaboration with
Didier Design Studio and Lake Flato
Location: State College, Pennsylvania, USA
Average summer high +27.3 °C (81.1 °F);
winter low −6.4 °C (20.5 °F)
40° 48' 18" N
352 m (1154 ft) elevation
1055 mm (41.53 in) average yearly rainfall

ABOUT THE AUTHORS

CLAIRE TAKACS

Claire Takacs is a freelance photographer who has specialised in capturing gardens and landscapes around the world for the past twenty years. Her work features regularly in international magazines, including *Gardens Illustrated*. She has contributed to many books, and this is her fifth title, which she has photographed exclusively. Previous books include: the highly acclaimed and successful *Dreamscapes* (Hardie Grant), which she also authored, *Australian Dreamscapes* (Hardie Grant), *Windcliff; A Story of People, Plants, and Gardens* by Dan Hinkley (Timber Press) and *Wild: The Naturalistic Garden*, with text by Noel Kingsbury (Phaidon).

GIACOMO GUZZON

Giacomo Guzzon is a landscape architect and expert in planting design. He has taught planting design at several schools and universities, such as Sheffield, Greenwich and KLC, and currently serves as Head of Planting Design at the international landscape architecture firm Gillespies in London. He contributes to conferences and publications and has spoken in Hong Kong, the US, and throughout Europe. He is currently pursuing a PhD in plant science at the Technical University of Berlin.

ACKNOWLEDGEMENTS

Firstly, thanks to Pam Brewster, for believing and putting complete trust in me to create another book. For your gentle and wise guidance, and your publishing expertise, which allowed for and brought out the best in *Visionary*.

Giacomo Guzzon, thank you for a brilliant collaboration to co-create and write this unique and timely book. I know you do and will continue to inspire important developments for our cities, today and into the future.

To my parents, Karl and Lyndsay Takacs, who let me live with them, yet again at 46, in Australia, as I spent eight months editing my images and forming this book together, with Hardie Grant. For your ever generous support and love over the years. And, Oliver, our beloved dog. Your presence, strongly felt as I worked; it seems you almost did this book with me. Urging me to get up from the computer, go for walks, to play, laugh and go outside to see rainbows.

Hilary Burden; you are a magician with words and a true friend. Thank you for your editing, extra writing, and research, all conducted with deep understanding, love, and your beautiful energy.

Thank you, Antonietta Anello, for your careful project editing and to the Design and Production team at Hardie Grant for working with me patiently and expertly, to create this beautiful book.

To every garden owner, designer and gardener. Thank you for sharing your remarkable and beautiful creations and for your hospitality, friendship and time communicating with us to help form the texts.

To you the reader, thank you for your support. This book is for you. I hope *Visionary* brings beauty, optimism, and inspiration.

Published in 2024 by Hardie Grant Books, an imprint of Hardie Grant Publishing

Hardie Grant Books (Melbourne)
Wurundjeri Country
Building 1, 658 Church Street
Richmond, Victoria 3121

Hardie Grant Books (London)
5th & 6th Floors
52–54 Southwark Street
London SE1 1UN

hardiegrant.com/books

Hardie Grant acknowledges the Traditional Owners of the Country on which we work, the Wurundjeri People of the Kulin Nation and the Gadigal People of the Eora Nation, and recognises their continuing connection to the land, waters and culture. We pay our respects to their Elders past and present.

 A catalogue record for this book is available from the National Library of Australia

Visionary: Gardens and Landscapes for Our Future
ISBN 9781743797624

10 9 8 7 6 5 4 3 2 1

Publishing Director: Pam Brewster
Project Editor: Antonietta Anello
Editors: Hilary Burden, Kate Daniel
Photographer and Photo Editor: Claire Takacs
Design Manager: Kristin Thomas
Designer: Celia Mance, Hardie Grant Design Studio
Head of production: Todd Rechner
Production Controller: Jessica Harvie

Colour reproduction by Splitting Image Colour Studio
Printed in China by Leo Paper Products LTD.

The paper this book is printed on is from FSC®-certified forests and other sources. FSC® promotes environmentally responsible, socially beneficial and economically viable management of the world's forests.